Recipe Collection

BEST-LOVED
RECIPES

Publications International, Ltd.

Louis Weber, CEO
Publications International, Ltd.
7373 North Cicero Avenue
Lincolnwood, IL 60712

Permission is never granted for commercial purposes.

Recipes developed and tested by the Land O'Lakes Test Kitchens. For questions regarding recipes in this cookbook or LAND O LAKES® products, call 1-800-328-4155.

Pictured on the front cover: Caramel 'n Chocolate Pecan Bars *(page 215).*
Pictured on the back cover: Hearty Beef Stew *(page 58),* Lemon Clove Cookie Sandwiches *(page 240)* and Potato, Ham & Cheese Bake *(page 20).*

ISBN-13: 978-1-4127-2832-4
ISBN-10: 1-4127-2832-0

Manufactured in China

8 7 6 5 4 3 2 1

Preparation and Cooking Times: All recipes were developed and tested in the Land O'Lakes Test Kitchens by professional home economists. Use "Preparation Time" and "Cooking, Baking, Microwaving or Broiling Time" given with each recipe as guides. Preparation time is based on the approximate amount of "active" time required to assemble the recipe. This includes steps such as chopping, mixing, cooking pasta, frosting, etc. Cooking, baking, microwaving or broiling times are based on the minimum amount of time required for these recipe steps.

CONTENTS

30

71

116

Lemon Pancakes with Berry Topping, p. 10

Quick Pineapple Rolls *(opposite page)*, p. 22

BREAKFAST AND BRUNCH

It's healthy to start the day off with a good breakfast, so why not make it delicious too? Treat your family to their favorite dishes to enjoy on a busy weekday or to savor during a leisurely weekend brunch.

Crunchy Snickerdoodle French Toast

Preparation time: **15 minutes** | Baking time: **15 minutes** | **6 servings**

- 1¼ cups LAND O LAKES™ Fat Free Half & Half or milk
- 3 eggs, slightly beaten
- 2 tablespoons sugar
- 1 teaspoon ground cinnamon
- 1 teaspoon vanilla
- 5 cups cinnamon-sugar crispy sweetened whole wheat and rice cereal, crushed*
- 12 (¾-inch thick) slices French bread

LAND O LAKES® Butter
Maple syrup, if desired

• Grease 15×10×1-inch jelly-roll pan. Combine half & half, eggs, sugar, cinnamon and vanilla in shallow bowl; mix well.

• Place crushed cereal in another shallow bowl. Dip bread slices in egg mixture then into cereal crumbs. Place into prepared pan. Cover; freeze until firm (1 to 2 hours or overnight).

• Heat oven to 425°F. Bake uncovered, turning once, for 15 to 20 minutes or until golden brown. Serve with butter and maple syrup, if desired.

*Substitute any cinnamon-flavored cereal or plain flake cereal.

tip:

The amount of egg mixture absorbed when making French toast depends upon the bread being used. Soft bread with an open, porous texture will absorb more liquid and absorb it more quickly than drier bread with a fine texture. Once you've dipped the first 1 or 2 slices, you can determine how long to keep the bread in the egg mixture, so you don't run out of the egg mixture.

Creamy Baked Oatmeal

Preparation time: **10 minutes** | Baking time: **40 minutes** | **4 (1-cup) servings**

Oatmeal

- 3 cups milk
- 2 eggs, beaten
- 3 tablespoons LAND O LAKES® Butter, melted
- ½ cup firmly packed brown sugar
- 1 teaspoon vanilla or ¼ teaspoon almond extract
- ¼ teaspoon salt
- 2 cups uncooked old-fashioned oats*
- 1 teaspoon ground cinnamon
- ½ cup sweetened dried cranberries or cherries

Toppings

- ½ cup slivered almonds, toasted, if desired
- Milk, LAND O LAKES® Butter, brown sugar or maple syrup, if desired

• Combine all oatmeal ingredients except oats, cinnamon and cranberries in large bowl. Add oats and cinnamon; stir until combined. Pour into greased 2-quart casserole; cover. Refrigerate 8 hours or overnight.

• Heat oven to 350°F. Add cranberries; stir. Bake, uncovered, for 40 to 50 minutes, stirring twice, until thick and creamy. Remove from oven; stir before serving.

• Sprinkle with almonds, if desired. Serve immediately with additional milk, butter, brown sugar or maple syrup, if desired.

*Substitute quick-cooking oats. Do not refrigerate. Bake immediately after combining all oatmeal ingredients.

tip:
To toast almonds, place onto baking sheet. Bake at 350°F. for 8 to 10 minutes, stirring occasionally, until golden brown.

Lemon Pancakes with Berry Topping

Preparation time: **20 minutes** | Cooking time: **2 minutes per pancake** | **6 (2-pancake) servings**

Pancakes

- 2 cups all-purpose baking mix
- 3 tablespoons sugar
- ½ cup milk
- 1 (6-ounce) container lemon-flavored yogurt
- 2 eggs
- 2 tablespoons LAND O LAKES® Butter, melted
- 2 tablespoons lemon juice

Topping

- ½ cup red currant jelly
- 2 cups fresh strawberries, halved*
- 1 cup fresh or frozen blueberries, thawed

- Combine all pancake ingredients in medium bowl until smooth.

- Heat lightly greased griddle or frying pan to 350°F. or until drops of water sizzle. For each pancake, spoon about ¼ cup batter onto hot griddle; spread to form 4-inch circle. Cook until bubbles form on top (1 to 2 minutes). Turn pancakes; continue cooking until browned (1 to 2 minutes). Keep warm. Repeat with remaining batter.

- Meanwhile, melt jelly in 2-quart saucepan over medium-low heat (2 to 3 minutes). Remove from heat. Add strawberries and blueberries; stir gently to coat. Serve over warm pancakes.

*Substitute 2 cups frozen strawberries, thawed.

tip:
For more lemon flavor, add 1 tablespoon freshly grated lemon peel to pancake batter.

Deep-Dish Breakfast Pizza

Preparation time: **30 minutes** | Baking time: **35 minutes** | **6 servings**

> 3 tablespoons LAND O LAKES® Butter
> 2 cups sliced onions
> 1 (10-ounce) can refrigerated pizza crust
> 4 ounces (1 cup) LAND O LAKES® Swiss Cheese, shredded
> 1 (10-ounce) package frozen chopped spinach, thawed, squeezed dry
> 4 slices crisply cooked bacon, crumbled
> 2 tablespoons chopped red bell pepper
> 3 eggs, beaten
> ¾ cup milk
> ¼ teaspoon pepper

• Heat oven to 350°F. Spray 9-inch pie pan with no-stick cooking spray; set aside.

• Melt butter in 12-inch nonstick skillet until sizzling; add onions. Cook over medium heat, stirring occasionally, until onions are deep golden brown (15 to 20 minutes).

• Meanwhile, pat or roll pizza crust into 11-inch circle on lightly floured surface. Place into prepared pie pan. Fold under excess dough; pinch edges.

• Mix ½ cup cheese and spinach in small bowl. Layer cooked onions, spinach mixture, bacon and red bell pepper over bottom of crust.

• Combine eggs, milk and pepper in small bowl; mix well. Pour egg mixture over spinach. Sprinkle with remaining cheese. Bake for 35 to 45 minutes or until eggs are set 2 inches from edges. Let stand 10 minutes before serving.

Bagel Strata with Spinach & Roasted Peppers

Preparation time: **30 minutes** | Baking time: **55 minutes** | **10 servings**

  2 cups milk

  6 eggs

  ½ teaspoon salt

  ¼ teaspoon pepper

  1 cup sliced fresh mushrooms

  6 ounces (1½ cups) LAND O LAKES® Swiss or Cheddar Cheese, shredded

  1 (10-ounce) package frozen chopped spinach, thawed, well-drained*

  1 (7-ounce) jar (⅔ cup) roasted red peppers, chopped, well-drained

  3 plain bagels (6 cups), split, cut into small bite-sized pieces

  2 tablespoons chopped onion

• Beat milk, eggs, salt and pepper in large bowl with wire whisk until well beaten. Add all remaining ingredients; mix well. Pour into greased 13×9-inch baking dish or pan. Cover; refrigerate 3 hours or overnight.

• Heat oven to 350°F. Bake, uncovered, for 55 to 60 minutes or until puffed and golden brown and knife inserted near center comes out clean. Let stand 5 minutes before serving.

• To serve, cut strata into squares.

*Substitute 1 (10-ounce) package frozen chopped broccoli, thawed, drained.

tip:
_____

To thaw chopped spinach in the microwave, cut slit in top of box or package. Microwave on DEFROST (30% power) for 5 to 6 minutes or until thawed.

Chocolate Sticky Rolls

Preparation time: **30 minutes** | Baking time: **20 minutes** | 16 rolls

Caramel

¼ cup LAND O LAKES® Butter, melted
2 tablespoons milk chocolate chips
¾ cup firmly packed brown sugar
2 tablespoons light corn syrup

Filling

¾ cup milk chocolate chips
¼ teaspoon ground cinnamon
3 tablespoons milk

Rolls

2 (1-pound) loaves frozen bread dough, thawed
½ cup chopped pecans

• Place butter and 2 tablespoons chocolate chips in medium microwave-safe bowl. Microwave on HIGH (100% power) until butter is melted (45 to 50 seconds). Stir until chocolate chips are completely melted. Stir in brown sugar and corn syrup; mix well. Spread onto bottom of greased 13×9-inch baking pan; set aside.

• Place all filling ingredients in small microwave-safe bowl. Microwave on HIGH until chocolate chips are almost melted (45 to 60 seconds). Stir until chocolate chips are melted and mixture is smooth.

• Roll out each bread dough loaf on lightly floured surface into 14×10-inch rectangle. Spread half of filling (about ⅓ cup) on each dough rectangle; sprinkle each with ¼ cup pecans. Roll each rectangle up jelly-roll fashion beginning with 14-inch side. Pinch edge of dough into roll to seal well. Cut each roll into 8 slices. Place dough slices, cut-side down, into prepared pan. Cover; let rise in warm place until double in size (45 to 60 minutes).

• Heat oven to 375°F. Bake for 20 to 25 minutes or until golden brown. Let stand 5 minutes. Invert pan onto serving platter; remove pan.

Butter Toffee Brunch Cake

Preparation time: **20 minutes** | Baking time: **35 minutes** | **15 servings**

½ cup LAND O LAKES® Butter, softened
½ cup sugar
½ cup firmly packed brown sugar
2 cups all-purpose flour
1 cup buttermilk*
1 egg
1 teaspoon baking soda
1 teaspoon vanilla
½ cup chopped nuts
¾ cup English toffee bits**

• Heat oven to 350°F. Grease and flour 13×9-inch baking pan.

• Combine butter, sugar and brown sugar in large bowl. Beat at medium speed, scraping bowl often, until creamy. Reduce speed to low; add flour. Beat until well mixed. Reserve ½ cup for topping.

• Add buttermilk, egg, baking soda and vanilla to remaining flour mixture. Continue beating until well mixed.

• Pour batter into prepared baking pan. Combine reserved flour mixture, nuts and toffee in medium bowl; sprinkle over batter. Bake for 35 to 40 minutes or until toothpick inserted in center comes out clean.

*Substitute 1 tablespoon vinegar or lemon juice plus enough milk to equal 1 cup. Let stand 10 minutes.
**Substitute 5 (1.4-ounce) chocolate-coated toffee candy bars, finely crushed. Freezing the candy bars makes them easier to crush.

Potato, Ham & Cheese Bake

Preparation time: **10 minutes** | Baking time: **35 minutes** | **6 servings**

    2 cups frozen shredded hash brown potatoes, thawed
    1 cup milk
    4 eggs
    ¼ teaspoon pepper
    1 cup cubed cooked ham
    ¼ cup sliced green onions
    ¼ cup chopped red bell pepper
    4 ounces (1 cup) LAND O LAKES® Cheddar Cheese, shredded

• Heat oven to 375°F. Press potatoes onto bottom and up sides of greased 9-inch glass pie pan. Bake for 10 minutes.

• Combine milk, eggs and pepper in medium bowl; beat until well mixed. Stir in ham, 2 tablespoons green onions and 2 tablespoons red bell pepper. Sprinkle half of cheese over potatoes. Pour egg mixture over cheese.

• Bake for 35 to 40 minutes or until knife inserted in center comes out clean. Top with remaining cheese, green onions and red bell pepper. Let stand 10 minutes before serving.

Breakfast Coolers

Preparation time: **5 minutes** | Freezing time: **2 hours (optional)** | 6 (¾-cup) servings

Peaches 'n Cream Cooler

2 cups frozen peach slices
1 cup LAND O LAKES™ Fat Free Half & Half
2 (11.5- to 12-ounce) cans peach nectar, chilled*
1 teaspoon vanilla

• Place all ingredients in 5-cup blender container. Cover; blend until smooth. Pour into glasses.

Pineapple-Banana Cooler

2 small bananas
1 cup LAND O LAKES™ Fat Free Half & Half
3 cups pineapple juice, chilled*

• Cut bananas into large chunks; wrap in aluminum foil. Freeze at least 2 hours or overnight.

• Place frozen bananas and all remaining ingredients in 5-cup blender container. Cover; blend until smooth. Pour into glasses.

Orange-Banana-Strawberry Cooler

2 bananas
2 cups orange juice
1 cup frozen whole unsweetened strawberries
1 cup LAND O LAKES™ Fat Free Half & Half

• Cut bananas into large chunks; wrap in aluminum foil. Freeze at least 2 hours or overnight.

• Place frozen bananas and all remaining ingredients in 5-cup blender container. Cover; blend until smooth. Pour into glasses.

*Substitute 3 cups orange juice.

tip:
Garnish glasses with fresh fruit, such as strawberries, citrus fruit slices, pineapple wedges or maraschino cherries.

Quick Pineapple Rolls *(photo on page 5)*

Preparation time: **20 minutes** | Baking time: **25 minutes** | **12 rolls**

  1 (20-ounce) can pineapple slices in juice, reserve juice
  ¼ cup sugar
  ½ teaspoon ground cinnamon
  1 (11-ounce) package refrigerated breadsticks
  ⅓ cup chopped cashews*
  2 tablespoons firmly packed brown sugar
  2 tablespoons LAND O LAKES® Butter, melted

• Heat oven to 375°F. Drain 6 pineapple slices on paper towels; reserve ½ cup juice. Pat pineapple dry; cut in half. (Reserve remaining pineapple for another use.)

• Combine sugar and cinnamon in small bowl.

• Unroll breadstick dough; do not separate. Sprinkle cashews evenly over dough; lightly press into dough. Sprinkle 1 tablespoon sugar mixture over cashews. Cut dough at perforations.

• Combine reserved pineapple juice and brown sugar in ungreased 13×9-inch baking pan; spread evenly on bottom.

• For each roll, place 1 pineapple slice half at end of dough strip; roll up. (Pineapple will not be completely covered with dough.) Pinch end to seal. Place rolls in prepared pan, seam-side down.

• Brush rolls and pineapple with melted butter; sprinkle with remaining sugar mixture. Bake for 25 to 30 minutes or until dark golden brown. Let stand at least 5 minutes. Serve warm.

*Substitute ⅓ cup chopped pecans.

tip:
These rolls are best if made close to serving time so they can be enjoyed fresh and warm.

Mocha Java

Preparation time: **10 minutes** | **6 (1⅓-cup) servings**

    6 cups strong hot coffee
    1 cup instant hot cocoa mix
    ¼ cup sugar
    2 cups LAND O LAKES™ Fat Free Half & Half

       LAND O LAKES™ Heavy Whipping Cream, whipped, sweetened, if desired
       Chocolate shavings, if desired

• Pour coffee into 3-quart saucepan; stir in cocoa mix and sugar until dissolved. Add half & half. Cook over medium heat, stirring occasionally, until heated through (3 to 4 minutes).

• Dollop each serving with whipped cream; sprinkle with chocolate shavings, if desired.

Best-Loved Blueberry Muffins, p. 30

Apple-Nut Coffee Cake *(opposite page)*, p. 32

MUFFINS AND QUICK BREADS

Just right for a portable breakfast, lunchbox addition or dinner bread basket, this selection of sweet and savory muffins, biscuits and breads is easy to make and enjoy anywhere.

Good Morning Muffins

Preparation time: **25 minutes** | Baking time: **20 minutes** | **12 muffins**

- ½ cup firmly packed brown sugar
- ¼ cup LAND O LAKES® Butter, softened
- 1 cup LAND O LAKES® Sour Cream
- 2 eggs
- ½ cup sweetened flaked coconut
- ½ cup raisins
- 2 medium (1 cup) carrots, shredded
- 1½ cups all-purpose flour
- 1 teaspoon baking soda
- 1 teaspoon ground cinnamon

- Heat oven to 375°F. Combine sugar and butter in large bowl. Beat at medium speed, scraping bowl often, until creamy. Add sour cream and eggs. Continue beating until well mixed. Stir in coconut, raisins and carrots by hand.

- Add flour, baking soda and cinnamon to sour cream mixture; stir just until moistened.

- Spoon batter into 12 greased or paper-lined muffin cups. Bake for 20 to 25 minutes or until lightly browned.

variations:

Prepare muffins as directed above. Bake as directed below.

Texas-Size Muffins: Spoon batter into greased Texas-size muffin pan. Bake for 28 to 32 minutes or until lightly browned. 6 muffins.

Mini Muffins: Spoon batter into greased mini muffin pans. Bake for 15 to 18 minutes or until lightly browned. 32 muffins.

Muffin Tops: Spoon batter into greased muffin-top pan. Bake for 14 to 18 minutes or until lightly browned. 8 muffin tops.

Mini Loaves: Spoon batter into 2 greased (5¾×3-inch) mini loaf pans. Bake for 32 to 37 minutes or until toothpick inserted in center comes out clean. 2 mini loaves.

Oat Bran Popovers with Herb Butter

Preparation time: **15 minutes** | Baking time: **35 minutes** | 6 popovers; ⅓ cup herb butter

Herb Butter

- ⅓ cup LAND O LAKES® Butter, softened
- 1 teaspoon finely chopped fresh oregano leaves*
- 1 teaspoon chopped fresh parsley

Popovers

- 3 eggs
- 1¼ cups milk
- 1 tablespoon LAND O LAKES® Butter, melted
- 1 cup all-purpose flour
- ¼ cup oat bran
- ¼ teaspoon salt

• Heat oven to 450°F. Stir together all herb butter ingredients in small bowl. Cover; refrigerate until serving time.

• Beat eggs in small bowl at medium speed, scraping bowl often, until thick and lemon-colored. Add milk and 1 tablespoon butter; continue beating 1 minute. Add flour, oat bran and salt; continue beating until well mixed. Pour batter into well-greased popover pan or 6-ounce custard cups. Bake for 15 minutes.

• Reduce oven temperature to 350°F. (DO NOT OPEN OVEN DOOR.) Bake for 20 to 25 minutes or until golden brown.

• Insert knife into popovers to allow steam to escape. Serve immediately with herb butter.

*Substitute ½ teaspoon dried oregano leaves, crushed.

tip:

Eggs and milk should be at room temperature to help ensure successful popovers.

Best-Loved Blueberry Muffins
Preparation time: **15 minutes** | Baking time: **22 minutes** | **12 muffins**

Muffin
  1 cup milk
  ½ cup LAND O LAKES® Butter, melted
  1 egg, slightly beaten
  2 cups all-purpose flour
  ⅓ cup sugar
  2 teaspoons baking powder
  1 teaspoon salt
  1 cup fresh or frozen blueberries

Topping
  ¼ cup LAND O LAKES® Butter, melted
  ¼ cup sugar

• Heat oven to 375°F. Combine milk, ½ cup melted butter and egg in large bowl. Add all remaining muffin ingredients except blueberries; stir just until moistened. Gently stir in blueberries.

• Spoon batter into greased or paper-lined 12-cup muffin pan. Bake for 22 to 26 minutes or until golden brown. Cool slightly; remove from pan.

• Dip tops of muffins in ¼ cup melted butter, then in sugar.

variations:

Lemon-Blueberry Muffins: Prepare muffins as directed, stirring in 1 tablespoon freshly grated lemon peel with flour. Bake as directed.
Raspberry-White Chocolate Chip Muffins: Omit blueberries. Add 1 cup fresh or frozen raspberries. Gently stir in ½ cup white baking chips with raspberries. Bake as directed.

tip:

Muffins can also be baked in nonstick Texas-size muffin pan. Bake for 27 to 32 minutes. Makes 6 muffins.

Apple-Nut Coffee Cake

Preparation time: **20 minutes** | Baking time: **30 minutes** | **15 servings**

Cake

2 cups all-purpose flour

1 cup sugar

½ cup LAND O LAKES® Sour Cream

½ cup LAND O LAKES® Butter, softened

¼ cup milk

2 eggs

1 teaspoon baking powder

1 teaspoon baking soda

1 teaspoon vanilla

¼ teaspoon salt

2 medium (2 cups) cooking apples, peeled, chopped*

Topping

½ cup chopped walnuts or pecans

½ cup firmly packed brown sugar

2 tablespoons LAND O LAKES® Butter, melted

1 teaspoon ground cinnamon

• Heat oven to 350°F. Combine all cake ingredients except apples in large bowl. Beat at medium speed, scraping bowl often, until smooth. Gently stir in apples by hand.

• Spread batter into greased 13×9-inch baking pan. Combine all topping ingredients in small bowl; sprinkle over batter. Bake for 30 to 35 minutes or until toothpick inserted in center comes out clean.

*Substitute 1 (16-ounce) can peaches, drained, chopped.

tip:
We recommend using Red Rome, Winesap, McIntosh or Haralson apples.

Maple French Toast Muffins

Preparation time: **30 minutes** | Baking time: **20 minutes** | **12 muffins**

French Toast Topping

- 3 tablespoons milk
- 1 egg, slightly beaten
- 6 slices (3½ cups) cinnamon swirl bread, crusts trimmed, cut into ½-inch cubes

Muffins

- 1 cup milk
- ½ cup LAND O LAKES® Butter, melted
- 1 egg, slightly beaten
- 1 teaspoon maple flavoring
- 2 cups all-purpose flour
- ¾ cup firmly packed brown sugar
- 2 teaspoons baking powder
- ½ teaspoon salt

Topping

- ¼ cup maple-flavored syrup
- 2 tablespoons sugar
- ¼ teaspoon ground cinnamon

• Heat oven to 375°F. Combine all French toast topping ingredients in medium bowl; set aside.

• Combine 1 cup milk, melted butter, 1 egg and maple flavoring in another medium bowl. Combine all remaining muffin ingredients in large bowl. Stir milk mixture into flour mixture just until mixed.

• Spoon batter into greased 12-cup muffin pan. Spoon French toast topping evenly over batter; press down slightly. Bake for 20 to 25 minutes or until toothpick inserted in center comes out clean.

• Immediately brush muffins with maple-flavored syrup. Combine sugar and cinnamon in small bowl. Sprinkle over glazed muffins. Cool 5 minutes; remove from pan. Serve warm.

tip:

Serve these muffins warm with maple-flavored butter. Combine ½ cup LAND O LAKES® Butter, softened, with 2 tablespoons firmly packed brown sugar and ¼ teaspoon maple flavoring in small bowl. Beat at medium speed until creamy. Store covered in refrigerator up to 3 weeks.

Cheddar Dill Scones

Preparation time: **20 minutes** | Baking time: **15 minutes** | **16 scones**

   2½ cups all-purpose flour
   4 ounces (1 cup) LAND O LAKES® Cheddar Cheese, shredded
   ¼ cup chopped fresh parsley
   1 tablespoon baking powder
   2 teaspoons dried dill weed
   ½ teaspoon salt
   ¾ cup LAND O LAKES® Butter
   ½ cup LAND O LAKES™ Half & Half
   2 eggs, slightly beaten

      LAND O LAKES® Cheddar Cheese, shredded, if desired

• Heat oven to 400°F. Combine flour, 1 cup cheese, parsley, baking powder, dill weed and salt in medium bowl; cut in butter with pastry blender or fork until mixture resembles coarse crumbs. Stir in half & half and eggs just until moistened.

• Turn dough onto lightly floured surface; knead until smooth (1 minute). Divide dough in half; roll each half into 8-inch circle. Cut each circle into 8 wedges. Place 1 inch apart onto greased baking sheets. Sprinkle with additional cheese, if desired. Bake for 15 to 20 minutes or until lightly browned.

Baking Powder Biscuit Muffins

Preparation time: **20 minutes** | Baking time: **14 minutes** | **18 muffins**

2½ cups all-purpose flour
¼ cup sugar
4 teaspoons baking powder
¾ cup cold LAND O LAKES® Butter
1 cup milk

LAND O LAKES® Butter
Jam or preserves, if desired

• Heat oven to 400°F. Combine flour, sugar and baking powder in large bowl; cut in butter with pastry blender or fork until mixture resembles coarse crumbs. Stir in milk just until moistened.

• Spoon 2 tablespoons batter into each paper-lined or greased muffin pan cup. Bake for 14 to 18 minutes or until lightly browned. Serve warm with butter and jam or preserves.

Roasted Red Pepper Biscuits

Preparation time: **30 minutes** | Baking time: **10 minutes** | **8 biscuits**

- 1 tablespoon LAND O LAKES® Butter
- ½ cup chopped red bell pepper
- ½ teaspoon finely chopped fresh garlic
- 2¼ cups all-purpose flour
- 1 tablespoon baking powder
- ¼ teaspoon salt
- ⅔ cup LAND O LAKES® Butter
- ⅔ cup buttermilk*

- 1 tablespoon LAND O LAKES® Butter, melted

• Heat oven to 425°F. Heat 1 tablespoon butter in 8-inch skillet until sizzling; add red bell pepper and garlic. Cook over medium heat, stirring occasionally, until crisply tender (3 to 5 minutes); set aside.

• Combine flour, baking powder and salt in large bowl; cut in ⅔ cup butter with pastry blender or fork until mixture resembles coarse crumbs. Add red bell pepper mixture and buttermilk; stir just until moistened.

• Turn dough onto lightly floured surface; knead until smooth (1 minute). Roll out dough to ¾-inch thickness. Cut out biscuits with 2½-inch biscuit cutter.

• Place biscuits 1 inch apart onto ungreased baking sheet. Brush tops with melted butter. Bake for 10 to 12 minutes or until lightly browned.

*Substitute 2 teaspoons vinegar or lemon juice plus enough milk to equal ⅔ cup. Let stand 10 minutes.

Holiday Orange Nut Bread

Preparation time: **25 minutes** | Baking time: **35 minutes** | **40 servings (5 mini loaves)**; ¾ cup orange marmalade butter

Bread

1½	cups sugar
1	cup LAND O LAKES® Butter, softened
4	eggs
1	cup LAND O LAKES® Sour Cream
½	cup orange juice
2	tablespoons freshly grated orange peel
3½	cups all-purpose flour
1½	teaspoons baking powder
1	teaspoon baking soda
2	cups chopped walnuts

Orange Marmalade Butter

½	cup LAND O LAKES® Butter, softened
1	tablespoon powdered sugar
3	tablespoons orange marmalade

• Heat oven to 350°F. Grease bottom only of 5 (5¾×3-inch) mini loaf pans; set aside.

• Combine sugar and 1 cup butter in large bowl. Beat at medium speed, scraping bowl often, until creamy. Add eggs; continue beating until well mixed. Add sour cream, orange juice and orange peel; continue beating until well mixed. Reduce speed to low; add flour, baking powder and baking soda. Beat until well mixed. Gently stir in nuts.

• Divide batter evenly among prepared pans. Bake for 35 to 45 minutes or until toothpick inserted in center comes out clean. Let stand 10 minutes; remove from pans. Cool completely.

• Meanwhile, combine all orange marmalade butter ingredients in small bowl. Beat at medium speed, scraping bowl often, until creamy. Cover; refrigerate until serving time.

variations:

Orange Walnut Poppy Seed Bread: Stir 2 tablespoons poppy seed into batter with walnuts. Bake as directed.

Orange Date Pecan Bread: Omit walnuts. Stir 2 cups chopped dates and 1 cup chopped pecans into batter. Bake as directed.

Orange Coconut Macadamia Nut Bread: Omit walnuts. Stir 1 cup sweetened flaked coconut and ⅔ cup coarsely chopped macadamia nuts into batter. Bake as directed.

Fruitcake Bread: Reduce walnuts to 1 cup. Combine ½ cup of the flour with 2 cups chopped candied cherry-pineapple mix in medium bowl; stir to coat. Substitute ½ cup brandy or rum* for ½ cup orange juice. Stir candied fruit mixture into batter. Bake as directed.

*Substitute 2 tablespoons brandy or rum extract. Pour extract into measuring cup and fill to ½ cup with orange juice.

tip:

Bread can also be baked in 2 (9×5-inch) loaf pans. Bake for 45 to 55 minutes or until toothpick inserted in center comes out clean.

tip:

For easier slicing, wrap breads tightly in foil or plastic food wrap and store overnight.

Golden Pumpkin Bread

Preparation time: **15 minutes** | Baking time: **30 minutes** | **24 servings (3 mini loaves)**

1½ cups all-purpose flour
  1 cup firmly packed brown sugar
  1 cup canned pumpkin
  ½ cup LAND O LAKES® Butter, softened
  2 eggs
1½ teaspoons ground cinnamon
  1 teaspoon baking powder
  1 teaspoon baking soda
  1 teaspoon salt
  ½ teaspoon ground ginger
  ¼ teaspoon ground cloves

• Heat oven to 350°F. Combine all ingredients in large bowl. Beat at medium speed, scraping bowl often, until well mixed.

• Spoon into 3 greased (5¾×3-inch) mini loaf pans. Bake for 30 to 35 minutes or until toothpick inserted in center comes out clean. Cool 10 minutes; remove from pan. Cool completely. Store refrigerated.

tip:
Bread can be baked in greased 9×5-inch loaf pan. Bake for 45 to 55 minutes or until toothpick inserted in center comes out clean.

Lemon & Pepper Drop Biscuits

Preparation time: **10 minutes** | Baking time: **15 minutes** | 10 biscuits

  2 cups all-purpose flour
  2 teaspoons baking powder
  1 teaspoon lemon & pepper seasoning
  1 teaspoon dried basil leaves
  ¼ teaspoon baking soda
  ½ cup LAND O LAKES® Butter, softened
  ¾ cup milk

  2 tablespoons LAND O LAKES® Butter, melted

• Heat oven to 375°F. Combine flour, baking powder, lemon & pepper, basil and baking soda in large bowl; mix in ½ cup butter with fork until mixture resembles coarse crumbs. Stir in milk just until moistened.

• Drop batter by ¼ cupfuls, 2 inches apart, onto large ungreased baking sheet. Brush tops with melted butter. Bake for 15 to 20 minutes or until golden brown. Serve warm.

Sour Cream Cornbread

Preparation time: **10 minutes** | Baking time: **22 minutes** | **8 servings**

- ¼ cup LAND O LAKES® Butter, softened
- 3 tablespoons sugar
- 2 eggs, slightly beaten
- ½ cup LAND O LAKES® Sour Cream
- ½ cup milk
- 1 cup all-purpose flour
- ⅔ cup yellow cornmeal
- 1½ teaspoons baking powder
- ½ teaspoon salt
- ¼ teaspoon baking soda

• Heat oven to 425°F. Combine butter and sugar in small bowl. Beat at medium speed, scraping bowl often, until creamy. Add eggs, 1 at a time, beating well after each addition. Stir in sour cream and milk. Add all remaining ingredients. Reduce speed to low; beat just until mixed.

• Pour batter into greased 8-inch cast-iron skillet. Bake for 22 to 26 minutes or until golden brown and toothpick inserted in center comes out clean. Serve warm.

tip:

This cornbread can be baked in a greased 8-inch square baking pan. Bake at 425°F. for 18 to 22 minutes.

tip:

Prepare batter as directed above. Spoon batter into 12 greased or paper-lined muffin cups. Bake for 15 to 18 minutes.

Walnut Banana Bread

Preparation time: **15 minutes** | Baking time: **1 hour** | **16 servings (1 loaf)**

>   ¾ cup sugar
>   ½ cup LAND O LAKES® Butter, softened
>   2 eggs
>   2 medium (1 cup) bananas, mashed
>   ½ teaspoon vanilla
> 1½ cups all-purpose flour
>   1 cup chopped walnuts
>   ½ teaspoon baking soda
>   ½ teaspoon salt
>   ¼ teaspoon ground cinnamon

• Heat oven to 350°F. Grease and flour 8×4-inch loaf pan; set aside.

• Combine sugar and butter in large bowl. Beat at medium speed, scraping bowl often, until creamy. Add eggs; continue beating until well mixed. Reduce speed to low; add banana and vanilla. Beat until well mixed. Stir in all remaining ingredients by hand.

• Spoon batter into prepared loaf pan. Bake for 60 to 70 minutes or until toothpick inserted in center comes out clean. Let stand 10 minutes; remove from pan. Cool completely.

tip:
For easy slicing, wrap in plastic food wrap and refrigerate overnight. This allows the crust to soften.

Hearty Beef Stew, p. 58

Curried Chicken Wild Rice Chowder *(opposite page)*, p. 56

SOUPS AND STEWS

Light lunch, first course or hearty supper, warm and tasty soups and stews simmering on the stove say "home-cooked" goodness to friends and family. So tell everyone that the soup's on!

Ham, Mac & Cheese Soup

Preparation time: **10 minutes** | Cooking time: **8 minutes** | **6 (1-cup) servings**

    4 ounces (1½ cups) uncooked dried small macaroni shells
    2 tablespoons LAND O LAKES® Butter
    2 tablespoons all-purpose flour
    1 teaspoon Dijon-style mustard
    1 (14-ounce) can chicken broth
1½ cups LAND O LAKES™ Fat Free Half & Half or milk
    1 (8-ounce) slice (1 inch thick) LAND O LAKES® Deli American Cheese, cut into
        1-inch cubes
    1 cup finely diced ham
        Salt and pepper, if desired

• Cook macaroni according to package directions; set aside.

• Melt butter in 3-quart saucepan until sizzling; stir in flour and mustard. Add broth and half & half. Cook over medium-high heat, stirring constantly, until mixture comes to a boil (4 to 5 minutes).

• Reduce heat to low; stir in cheese until melted. Stir in macaroni and ham. Cook until heated through (4 to 5 minutes). Salt and pepper to taste, if desired.

tip:
Try chopped or sliced hot dogs instead of ham.

Roasted Carrot Soup

Preparation time: **25 minutes** | Baking time: **35 minutes** | 8 (1-cup) servings

    2 pounds (5 cups) carrots, peeled, cut into ½-inch slices*
    1 large (16 ounces) yam, peeled, cut into ½-inch slices
    1 medium (1 cup) onion, cut into eighths
    4 whole cloves fresh garlic, peeled
    3 tablespoons olive or vegetable oil
    3 (14-ounce) cans chicken or vegetable broth
    1 cup LAND O LAKES™ Fat Free Half & Half or milk
    1 tablespoon fresh chopped thyme leaves**
       Salt and pepper, if desired

       Fresh thyme sprigs, if desired

• Heat oven to 350°F. Spray 15×10×1-inch jelly-roll pan with no-stick cooking spray.

• Place carrots, yam, onion and garlic in pan. Toss with oil. Bake for 35 to 45 minutes, stirring occasionally, until vegetables are tender.

• Place half of vegetable mixture, half of chicken broth and half & half in 5-cup blender container. Cover; process until smooth. Pour mixture into 4-quart saucepan. Repeat with remaining vegetable mixture, chicken broth and half & half.

• Stir in 1 tablespoon thyme. Season with salt and pepper, if desired. Cook, stirring occasionally, until soup is heated through (5 to 6 minutes).

• To serve, ladle soup into individual bowls; garnish with fresh thyme sprigs, if desired.

*Substitute 2 (1-pound) packages baby carrots.
**Substitute ¾ teaspoon dried thyme leaves.

tip:
Try this soup cold or at room temperature.

Red Pepper Asparagus Soup

Preparation time: **30 minutes** | Cooking time: **28 minutes** | 8 (1-cup) servings

Soup

- 3 tablespoons LAND O LAKES® Butter
- 1½ pounds (about 5 cups) asparagus, ends trimmed, cut into ½-inch pieces
- 2 medium (1 cup) red potatoes, peeled, coarsely chopped
- 1 leek (¾ cup), rinsed, thinly sliced*
- 1 medium (1 cup) red bell pepper, coarsely chopped
- 1 teaspoon finely chopped garlic
- 2 (14-ounce) cans vegetable broth
- 1 tablespoon balsamic vinegar or soy sauce
- 1 tablespoon finely chopped fresh tarragon leaves**
- 2 cups LAND O LAKES™ Fat Free Half & Half or milk
- 1 teaspoon salt
- ¼ teaspoon pepper

Topping

- ½ cup LAND O LAKES® Sour Cream
- ½ teaspoon chopped fresh tarragon leaves***

• Melt butter in 6-quart saucepan over medium-high heat until sizzling; add asparagus, potatoes, leek, red bell pepper and garlic. Cook, stirring occasionally, until asparagus is crisply tender (10 to 12 minutes).

• Stir in vegetable broth, balsamic vinegar and 1 tablespoon tarragon. Continue cooking until asparagus is tender (10 to 12 minutes). Remove from heat; cool 10 minutes. Stir in half & half, salt and pepper.

• Place 2 cups soup in 5-cup blender container. Cover; blend until very smooth. Repeat with remaining soup, 2 cups at a time. Place soup in 4-quart saucepan. Cook over medium heat until soup is heated through (8 to 10 minutes).

• Combine sour cream and ½ teaspoon tarragon leaves. Top each serving with 1 tablespoon sour cream mixture.

*Substitute ¾ cup thinly sliced onion.
**Substitute 1 teaspoon crushed dried tarragon leaves.
***Substitute ⅛ teaspoon crushed dried tarragon leaves.

tip:
Use a dry measuring cup or ladle to scoop soup from saucepan to blender. After soup is puréed, pour it directly from blender container into 4-quart saucepan.

tip:
The smaller the leek, the more tender it will be. To cut leeks, trim roots and leafy ends. Split leeks from top to bottom; rinse thoroughly and slice. Store leeks in refrigerator up to 5 days in resealable plastic food storage bag.

Hearty Beef & Pasta Soup

Preparation time: **20 minutes** | Cooking time: **1 hour 3 minutes** | **8 (1⅓-cup) servings**

 4 ounces (1½ cups) uncooked dried rigatoni pasta
 1 tablespoon LAND O LAKES® Butter
 1 pound beef stew meat, cut into ½-inch pieces
 1 large onion, cut into eighths, separated
 1 teaspoon finely chopped fresh garlic
 2 medium (1 cup) carrots, sliced
 2 ribs (1 cup) celery, sliced
 3 (14-ounce) cans beef broth
 ½ teaspoon caraway seed
 ¼ teaspoon coarse ground pepper
 3 cups coarsely chopped cabbage
 1 (9-ounce) package (2 cups) frozen Italian green beans

• Cook rigatoni according to package directions. Drain; set aside.

• Meanwhile, melt butter in 5-quart saucepan until sizzling; stir in beef, onion and garlic. Cook over medium-high heat, stirring occasionally, until beef is lightly browned (4 to 6 minutes).

• Add all remaining ingredients, except rigatoni, cabbage and green beans. Continue cooking until mixture comes to a full boil (8 to 10 minutes). Cover; reduce heat to medium-low. Cook, stirring occasionally, until beef is tender (40 to 50 minutes).

• Add cabbage. Continue cooking, stirring occasionally, until cabbage is slightly softened (5 to 8 minutes). Add cooked rigatoni and green beans. Continue cooking, stirring occasionally, until rigatoni and green beans are heated through (6 to 8 minutes).

Curried Chicken Wild Rice Chowder

Preparation time: **20 minutes** | Cooking time: **8 hours** | **10 (1-cup) servings**

Chowder

- 1 pound boneless skinless chicken breast halves, cut into 1-inch pieces
- 1 cup uncooked wild rice, rinsed
- 1 cup frozen whole kernel corn
- 1 medium (½ cup) carrot, shredded
- 1 medium (½ cup) onion, chopped
- 1 rib (½ cup) celery, chopped
- 2 tablespoons chopped fresh parsley*
- 3 (14-ounce) cans chicken broth
- 2 teaspoons curry powder
- 3 cups LAND O LAKES™ Fat Free Half & Half or milk
- 2 tablespoons all-purpose flour
  Salt and pepper, if desired

Garnish

Sliced or slivered almonds, toasted, if desired

Chopped fresh parsley, if desired

- Combine all chowder ingredients except half & half, flour, salt and pepper in slow cooker.

- Cover; cook on Low heat setting for 8 to 10 hours or until chicken and rice are tender.

- Just before serving, increase heat setting to High. Combine half & half and flour in small bowl; whisk until smooth. Stir into chowder; cook, stirring occasionally, until heated through (6 to 10 minutes). Season with salt and pepper, if desired.

- To serve, spoon into individual serving bowls; sprinkle with almonds and parsley, if desired.

*Substitute 2 teaspoons dried parsley.

tip:
You can now purchase chicken broth in aseptic boxes. These are convenient because you can store leftover broth in the box in the refrigerator.

Hearty Beef Stew

Preparation time: **20 minutes** | Cooking time: **8 hours** | **4 (2-cup) servings**

    1   tablespoon LAND O LAKES® Butter
    ¾   pound beef stew meat, cut into bite-sized pieces
    1½ teaspoons finely chopped fresh garlic
    1   small (1¼ cups) sweet potato, cut into ¾-inch pieces
    1   medium parsnip, peeled, cut into ½-inch slices
    ½   pound baby Yukon Gold potatoes, cut into 1-inch pieces
    1   (14.5-ounce) can diced tomatoes
    1   (14 ounce) can beef broth
    ⅓   cup hoisin sauce
    1   teaspoon dried thyme leaves

• Melt butter in 10-inch skillet until sizzling; add beef and garlic. Cook over medium-high heat until beef is browned (4 to 5 minutes); drain off fat.

• Place browned beef and all remaining ingredients in slow cooker. Stir to mix well. Cover; cook on Low heat setting for 8 to 9 hours or until beef is tender.

tip:

Store leftover stew in resealable freezer containers or bags; freeze up to 3 months. To thaw, place in refrigerator for 24 hours. Reheat in microwave or over medium-low heat in 2-quart saucepan.

tip:

Parsnips are a root vegetable with a mild sweet flavor. They are commonly boiled and mashed like potatoes but in this entrée they add a sweet complement to the other vegetables in the stew. Nutritionally, they contain a small amount of iron and vitamin C.

tip:

Hoisin sauce, traditionally used in oriental cooking, has a sweet and spicy flavor. This sauce can be found in the Asian section of the supermarket. An opened jar should be stored in the refrigerator.

Sirloin Chili

Preparation time: **15 minutes** | Cooking time: **54 minutes** | 8 (1½-cup) servings

      3   tablespoons LAND O LAKES® Butter
    1½   pounds boneless beef sirloin, cut into 1-inch pieces
      2   large (2 cups) onions, chopped
      4   teaspoons finely chopped fresh garlic
      1   (28-ounce) can whole tomatoes, cut-up
      2   (15.5- to 16-ounce) cans dark red kidney beans, rinsed, drained
      1   (15.5-ounce) can Great Northern beans, rinsed, drained
      1   (14-ounce) can beef broth
      1   (11-ounce) can tomato juice
      2   tablespoons chili powder
      1   tablespoon dried basil leaves
      6   ounces (1½ cups) LAND O LAKES® Cheddar Cheese, cut into ½-inch cubes

• Melt 2 tablespoons butter in 6-quart saucepan until sizzling; add beef. Cook over medium-high heat, stirring occasionally, until browned (3 to 5 minutes). Remove beef.

• Melt remaining 1 tablespoon butter in same saucepan until sizzling; add onions and garlic. Cook over medium-high heat, stirring occasionally, until onion is softened (3 to 4 minutes). Add browned beef and all remaining ingredients except cheese. Continue cooking until mixture comes to a boil (4 to 6 minutes). Reduce heat to medium-low. Cover; cook 30 minutes. Uncover; continue cooking for 15 to 30 minutes or until desired consistency.

• Ladle into serving bowls. Sprinkle each serving with cheese cubes.

tip:
The fastest way to peel a clove of garlic is to put the flat side of the blade of a chef's knife over the garlic and smack the blade with the heel of your hand. The clove will crack and the skin will fall away. Finely chop the garlic as directed in your recipe.

Chicken Stew with Dumplings

Preparation time: **1 hour** | Cooking time: **1 hour 20 minutes** | 8 servings

Stew

2½ to 3 pounds chicken thighs

5 cups water

10 baby carrots, cut in half

2 ribs celery, cut into ¼-inch slices

1 medium onion, cut into eighths

1 (10-ounce) package frozen peas

1 teaspoon salt

⅛ teaspoon pepper

Dumplings

1½ cups all-purpose flour

2 teaspoons baking powder

¾ teaspoon salt

3 tablespoons LAND O LAKES® Butter, softened

¾ cup milk

¼ cup chopped fresh parsley

• Place chicken in 8-quart saucepan; cover with water. Cover; cook over medium heat until chicken is fork tender (50 to 60 minutes). Remove chicken from broth; skim fat. Remove chicken from bones; return to broth. Add all remaining stew ingredients. Cover; cook over medium heat until vegetables are fork tender (15 to 20 minutes).

• Combine flour, baking powder and salt in large bowl; cut in butter with pastry blender or fork until mixture resembles coarse crumbs. Stir in milk and parsley.

• Drop dumplings by rounded tablespoonfuls into hot stew. Cook, uncovered, 10 to 15 minutes. Cover; continue cooking until dumplings are tender (5 to 10 minutes).

Chunky Tomato Basil Soup

Preparation time: **10 minutes** | Cooking time: **7 minutes** | 8 (1¼-cup) servings

  2 (14-ounce) cans chicken broth
  1 (28-ounce) can diced tomatoes
  1 (26-ounce) jar tomato and basil pasta sauce*
  ½ cup LAND O LAKES™ Fat Free Half & Half or milk

  1 cup LAND O LAKES® Sour Cream
  2 tablespoons purchased pesto sauce

• Combine chicken broth, diced tomatoes and pasta sauce in 4-quart saucepan. Cook over high heat, stirring occasionally, until mixture comes to a full boil (5 to 7 minutes).

• Reduce heat to low; stir in half & half. Continue cooking until heated through (2 to 3 minutes). (DO NOT BOIL.)

• Combine sour cream and pesto in small bowl. To serve, ladle soup into individual serving bowls; top each with 2 tablespoons sour cream mixture.

*Substitute 1 jar of your favorite tomato-based pasta sauce and 1 teaspoon dried basil leaves.

Shrimp Salad Poor Boys, p. 71

Grilled Portabella Mushroom Burgers *(opposite page)*, p. 76

SANDWICHES

With its infinite variety of possible combinations, the versatile sandwich can be anything from a quick snack to a gourmet meal. This tasty collection of tempting choices has something for everyone.

Pepper Jack Burgers

Preparation time: **15 minutes** | Grilling time: **10 minutes** | **4 sandwiches**

  1½ pounds extra-lean ground beef
   2 tablespoons Worcestershire sauce
  ¼ teaspoon salt
  ¼ teaspoon freshly ground or coarse ground pepper
   2 ounces (½ cup) LAND O LAKES® Hot Pepper Jack Cheese, shredded
   3 tablespoons LAND O LAKES® Butter, softened
  1½ teaspoons chopped fresh chives
   4 onion-topped hamburger buns
   2 tablespoons LAND O LAKES® Butter, softened
  12 (¼-inch thick) slices LAND O LAKES® Hot Pepper Jack Cheese (from 8-ounce package)
      Lettuce leaves, if desired
      Tomato slices, if desired

• Heat gas grill on medium or charcoal grill until coals are ash white. Combine ground beef, Worcestershire sauce, salt and pepper in large bowl; mix lightly. Shape into 4 (½-inch thick) patties.

• Combine shredded cheese, 3 tablespoons butter and chives in small bowl; mix well. Shape cheese mixture into 4 equal-sized balls; flatten slightly. Press a small indentation into center of each beef patty. Place cheese balls into each indentation; form ground beef around cheese ball, pinching to seal well.

• Place patties onto grill. Grill, turning once, until internal temperature reaches at least 160°F. or until meat is no longer pink in center (10 to 14 minutes).

• Meanwhile, spread cut sides of buns with 2 tablespoons butter. Place onto grill, butter-side down. Grill until toasted. Top each burger with 3 slices cheese before removing from grill.

• To serve, place lettuce leaf onto bottom half of bun, if desired. Top with burger and tomato slices, if desired, and top half of bun.

tip:
Chill the prepared patties at least 30 minutes before grilling. This allows the butter mixture in the center to firm up, making it less likely to ooze out during grilling.

Grilled Fish Tacos

Preparation time: **30 minutes** | Grilling time: **10 minutes** | **4 servings**

Tacos

½ pound frozen cod or other mild whitefish fillets, thawed

1 tablespoon LAND O LAKES® Butter, melted

1 (1.25-ounce) package taco seasoning mix

½ cup LAND O LAKES® Sour Cream

2 tablespoons milk

8 hard corn taco shells or soft flour tortillas

4 ounces (1 cup) LAND O LAKES® Cheddar Cheese, shredded

Toppings

Chopped avocado, chopped tomatoes, shredded coleslaw mix, sliced green onions, as desired

• Heat gas grill on medium or charcoal grill until coals are ash white. Arrange cod fillets in single layer on heavy-duty aluminum foil. Brush with melted butter; sprinkle with 2 tablespoons taco seasoning, turning to coat.

• Place aluminum foil with cod onto grill. Grill until fish in no longer translucent and flakes easily with fork (10 to 12 minutes).

• Meanwhile, combine sour cream, milk and remaining taco seasoning in small bowl. Heat taco shells as directed on package.

• To serve, break fish into bite-sized chunks; place into taco shells. Sprinkle with cheese; add toppings, as desired. Drizzle with sour cream mixture.

tip:
Make a fish taco salad bowl. Toss all the taco ingredients into a serving bowl and crumble broken taco shells over the top.

Grilled Pepper Panini

Preparation time: **10 minutes** | Broiling time: **1 minute** | **6 sandwiches**

  2 tablespoons LAND O LAKES® Butter, softened
  2 teaspoons finely chopped fresh garlic
  6 (6-inch) French-style sandwich rolls, split
18 (⅛-inch) red, green and/or yellow bell pepper rings
  3 ounces (¾ cup) LAND O LAKES® Mozzarella Cheese, shredded
  2 tablespoons fresh oregano leaves*

• Heat broiler. Combine butter and garlic in small bowl.

• To assemble sandwiches, spread ½ teaspoon butter mixture onto cut side of each roll half. Place bottom halves of rolls onto ungreased baking sheet; top each with 3 bell pepper rings, cheese and 1 teaspoon oregano leaves.

• Broil 4 to 5 inches from heat until cheese is melted (1 to 1½ minutes).

*Substitute 2 teaspoons dried oregano leaves.

Shrimp Salad Poor Boys

Preparation time: **20 minutes** | **4 sandwiches**

⅓ cup seafood cocktail sauce
¼ cup LAND O LAKES® Sour Cream
¼ cup thinly sliced green onions
2 (5- to 7-ounce) packages frozen cooked salad shrimp, thawed
4 (7- to 8-inch) sandwich buns
1 cup shredded lettuce
1 medium tomato, thinly sliced

• Combine cocktail sauce and sour cream in medium bowl; mix well. Stir in green onions and shrimp.

• Split sandwich buns; scoop out center of bottom bun halves, leaving ¾-inch shell. Fill each bread shell with one-quarter shrimp mixture; top with lettuce, tomato and top half of bun.

French Onion Beef Brisket Sandwiches

Preparation time: **30 minutes** | Grilling time: **2 hours 50 minutes** | **10 sandwiches**

  1 tablespoon LAND O LAKES® Butter
  1 (2- to 3-pound) beef brisket
  3 large (about 3 cups) onions, halved, sliced
 ¼ cup apple juice
  2 cloves garlic, chopped
  1 (10.5-ounce) can condensed beef consommé
  1 tablespoon firmly packed brown sugar
  1 tablespoon balsamic vinegar
  1 teaspoon salt
10 kaiser rolls
10 (¾-ounce) slices LAND O LAKES® Deli Swiss Cheese

• Heat oven to 325°F. Melt butter in 12-inch skillet until sizzling; place brisket in skillet. Cook over medium-high heat, turning once, until browned (8 to 10 minutes).

• Meanwhile, combine all remaining ingredients except rolls and cheese in 13×9-inch baking pan. Place browned brisket over onion mixture; cover tightly with aluminum foil. Bake for 2½ to 3 hours or until meat is fork tender and internal temperature reaches 170°F.

• Place brisket onto cutting board; trim fat. Slice brisket across grain into thin slices; place beef slices onto bottom of kaiser rolls. Top each with onion mixture, cheese and bun tops. Spoon pan juices into cups for dipping.

tip:
Cook and slice brisket the day before you intend to serve it. To reheat, cover tightly with aluminum foil and heat in 350°F. oven until hot (30 to 35 minutes). Or place in microwave-safe dish. Cover with plastic food wrap; microwave on HIGH (100% power), stirring occasionally, for 3 to 5 minutes or until heated through.

Chili Burger with Sweet Potato Fries

Preparation time: **15 minutes** | Baking time: **20 minutes** | Cooking time: **10 minutes** | **4 servings**

Fries

- 2 tablespoons LAND O LAKES® Butter, melted
- 2 medium sweet potatoes, peeled, cut into ½-inch strips
- 1 teaspoon chili powder
- ¼ cup grated Parmesan cheese
- ¼ teaspoon salt
- ⅛ teaspoon ground red pepper

Burgers

- 1 pound lean ground beef
- ¼ cup finely chopped onion
- 2 tablespoons chili sauce
- ½ teaspoon pepper
- ¼ teaspoon salt
- 1 tablespoon LAND O LAKES® Butter
- 4 (¾-ounce) slices LAND O LAKES® Deli American Cheese

- 4 hamburger buns, if desired

• Heat oven to 425°F. Place melted butter into large bowl; add sweet potatoes. Toss to coat. Add all remaining fries ingredients; toss to coat sweet potatoes. Arrange sweet potatoes in single layer on greased 15×10×1-inch baking pan. Bake for 20 to 25 minutes, turning sweet potatoes once, until golden brown.

• Meanwhile, combine ground beef, onion, chili sauce, pepper and salt in large bowl; mix well. Form mixture into 4 (4-inch) patties. Melt 1 tablespoon butter in large skillet until sizzling; add patties. Cook over medium-high heat, turning once, to desired doneness (10 to 12 minutes). Top each burger with 1 slice cheese. Serve on hamburger buns, if desired.

tip:
Sweet potato flesh can range from yellow to deep orange. The orange-fleshed varieties are generally sweeter and include the Garnet, Jewel and Beauregard varieties. Sweet potatoes are high in vitamins A and C and are a good source of potassium and fiber.

Grilled Portabella Mushroom Burgers

Preparation time: **10 minutes** | Grilling time: **7 minutes** | **2 sandwiches**

>   2 tablespoons LAND O LAKES® Butter, melted
>   1 tablespoon chopped fresh basil leaves*
>   2 teaspoons finely chopped fresh garlic
>   2 medium (about 4 inches in diameter) portabella mushrooms
>   2 onion slices
>   2 whole wheat hamburger buns, split
>   2 romaine lettuce leaves
>   2 slices tomato

• Heat gas grill to medium or charcoal grill until coals are ash white. Combine butter, basil and garlic in small bowl. Brush butter mixture over mushrooms, onion and cut sides of buns.

• Place mushrooms and onions onto grill. Grill, turning once and brushing with remaining butter mixture, until mushrooms are tender (6 to 8 minutes).

• Place buns onto grill, cut-side down. Grill until toasted (1 to 2 minutes).

• To serve, place lettuce onto grilled bun bottoms. Place 1 grilled mushroom, tomato and grilled onion slice onto each bottom half of bun. Cover with top half of bun.

*Substitute ¾ teaspoon dried basil leaves.

broiling directions:

Heat broiler. Brush butter mixture over mushrooms, onion and cut sides of buns. Place mushrooms and onions on broiler pan. Broil 6 to 8 inches from heat, turning once and brushing with remaining butter mixture, until mushrooms are tender (6 to 8 minutes). Place buns on broiler pan, cut-side up. Broil 6 to 8 inches from heat until toasted (1 to 2 minutes).

Easy Stromboli

Preparation time: **15 minutes** | Baking time: **20 minutes** | **6 servings**

Sandwich

Cornmeal

1 (11-ounce) tube refrigerated French bread loaf

1 teaspoon Italian seasoning*

4 ounces thinly sliced ham

2 ounces thinly sliced Genoa salami

½ (10-ounce) package frozen cut spinach, thawed, well-drained

6 ounces (1½ cups) LAND O LAKES® Mozzarella Cheese, shredded

⅓ cup chopped ripe olives

1 egg, beaten

1 teaspoon water

Sauce

1 cup marinara sauce

• Heat oven to 350°F. Grease large baking sheet; sprinkle with cornmeal; set aside.

• Unroll French bread loaf on lightly floured surface. Cut into 2 (12×6-inch) rectangles. Sprinkle Italian seasoning over both rectangles. Top each rectangle with ham, salami, spinach, cheese and olives.

• Roll up each rectangle jelly-roll fashion, starting at 1 long side; pinch seams to seal. Place onto prepared baking sheet, seam-side down. Cut 5 diagonal slices across top of each roll. Combine egg and water in small bowl. Brush tops of each roll. Bake for 20 to 25 minutes or until browned and thoroughly heated.

• Heat marinara sauce in 1-quart saucepan over medium heat until warm (2 to 3 minutes). Cut each roll into slices. Serve warm with marinara sauce.

*Substitute ¼ teaspoon each dried basil leaves, dried marjoram leaves and dried oregano leaves and ⅛ teaspoon rubbed sage.

tip:

Salamis vary greatly in size, shape and seasonings. Genoa salami is made from pork and veal. It's boldly seasoned with pepper, garlic and red wine and has a texture similar to that of pepperoni.

Open-Faced Turkey, Cranberry & Apple Sandwiches

Preparation time: **10 minutes** | Broiling time: **1 minute** | **4 sandwiches**

Bread

- 4 (about 7×3×½-inch) slices Italian artisan bread*
- 1 tablespoon LAND O LAKES® Butter, softened

Turkey Salad

- 2 cups chopped cooked turkey
- ¼ cup sweetened dried cranberries
- ¼ cup mayonnaise
- 1 small (½ cup) green apple, peeled, chopped
- 2 tablespoons finely chopped celery
- 1 tablespoon honey mustard
- 4 ounces (1 cup) LAND O LAKES® Chedarella® Cheese, shredded

• Heat broiler. Spread 1 side of each bread slice with butter. Place onto large ungreased baking sheet, butter-side up.

• Combine all turkey salad ingredients except cheese in medium bowl; mix well.

• Top each bread slice with about ¾ cup turkey mixture and ¼ cup cheese.

• Broil 4 to 6 inches from heat or until cheese is melted and light golden brown (1 to 2 minutes).

*Substitute 4 bagel halves.

Cheese-Topped Tuna Burgers

Preparation time: **10 minutes** | Cooking time: **6 minutes** | **6 sandwiches**

   2 (6-ounce) cans tuna in water, drained
   2 cups (36 to 40) crushed buttery round crackers
   1 rib (½ cup) celery, finely chopped
  ⅓ cup mayonnaise
  ½ teaspoon onion powder
   1 egg
   2 tablespoons LAND O LAKES® Butter
   6 (¾-ounce) slices LAND O LAKES® Deli American Cheese

   6 hamburger buns, toasted

• Combine tuna, 1 cup cracker crumbs, celery, mayonnaise, onion powder and egg in medium bowl. Shape mixture into 6 (4-inch) patties.

• Place remaining cracker crumbs into pie pan or shallow bowl. Lightly press both sides of tuna patties into cracker crumbs.

• Melt butter in 12-inch skillet until sizzling. Cook tuna patties over medium-high heat, carefully turning once, until golden brown (6 to 8 minutes). Top each with 1 slice cheese.

• Serve on hamburger buns.

tip:
Chunk light tuna is moister, softer in texture and darker in color than albacore tuna. Patties made with albacore tuna will be slightly firmer than those made with chunk light tuna.

Deep-Dish Chicken Pot Pie, p. 90

Pesto 'n Shrimp Risotto *(opposite page)*, p. 97

CASSEROLES AND ONE-DISH MEALS

Some days, nothing but comfort food will hit the spot. Make a warm and satisfying family favorite for lunch or dinner, and be ready to serve seconds.

Spicy Pork Enchiladas with Mole Sauce

Preparation time: **15 minutes** | Baking time: **20 minutes** | **8 servings**

Mole Sauce

- ½ cup chicken broth
- 1 (14.5-ounce) can diced tomatoes with mild green chiles
- 1 (1-ounce) square semi-sweet baking chocolate
- 1 teaspoon sugar
- ½ teaspoon ground cumin
- ½ teaspoon salt
- ¼ teaspoon pepper

Enchiladas

- 3 tablespoons LAND O LAKES® Butter
- 1 small (¼ cup) onion, finely chopped
- 1 pound cooked pork, shredded
- ⅛ teaspoon ground red pepper
- 8 (8-inch) flour tortillas
- 2 ounces (½ cup) LAND O LAKES® Co-Jack® or Chedarella® Cheese, shredded
- 2 ounces (½ cup) LAND O LAKES® Mozzarella Cheese, shredded

• Heat oven to 350°F. Combine all sauce ingredients in 2-quart saucepan. Cook over medium heat until mixture comes to a full boil (3 to 4 minutes). Cool slightly. Place mixture in 5-cup blender container or food processor bowl fitted with metal blade. Cover; blend 1 minute or until smooth; set aside.

• Melt butter in 10-inch skillet until sizzling; add onion. Cook over medium-high heat, stirring occasionally, until onion is softened (3 to 4 minutes). Stir in ½ cup mole sauce, shredded pork and ground red pepper; mix well.

• Divide pork mixture evenly among tortillas; roll up tortillas. Place into greased 13×9-inch baking dish, seam-side down. Pour remaining sauce over tortillas; sprinkle with cheeses. Bake for 20 to 25 minutes or until hot and bubbly.

tip:
Mole sauce is a rich reddish-brown Mexican sauce enhanced with a touch of chocolate.

tip:
Purchase already-cooked pork roast or cubes for shredded pork. Heat pork slightly for easier shredding.

Oriental-Style Beef & Noodles

Preparation time: **10 minutes** | Cooking time: **11 minutes** | **4 servings**

    2 tablespoons LAND O LAKES® Butter
    1 pound boneless beef sirloin, cut into thin bite-sized strips
    ¼ cup thick stir-fry sauce
    1 (14-ounce) can low-sodium beef broth
    2 tablespoons apricot or peach spreadable fruit
    ⅛ teaspoon ground red pepper
    4 ounces (about 2 cups) uncooked dried fine egg noodles
    1 (8-ounce) package (1½ cups) frozen sugar snap peas
    1 medium (1 cup) red or yellow bell pepper, coarsely chopped
    ¼ cup salted peanuts

• Melt butter in 12-inch skillet until sizzling; add beef strips. Cook over medium-high heat, stirring occasionally, until browned (3 to 4 minutes). Remove beef from skillet; keep warm.

• Add stir-fry sauce, broth, spreadable fruit and ground red pepper to same skillet. Cook over high heat until mixture comes to a boil (2 to 3 minutes). Stir in noodles. Cover; reduce heat to medium. Cook until noodles are tender (5 minutes).

• Stir in browned beef, sugar snap peas and bell pepper. Continue cooking, uncovered and stirring occasionally, until vegetables are crisply tender (2 to 3 minutes). Sprinkle with peanuts.

tip:
Shop for fresh bell peppers with bright colors and firm skin. Avoid any that feel soft, appear shriveled or have bruises. You can keep peppers covered and in the refrigerator for up to 5 days. For longer storage, slice or chop the peppers and place them in freezer bags in the freezer for up to 6 months.

Cheesy Scalloped Potatoes & Ham

Preparation time: **20 minutes** | Baking time: **1 hour 5 minutes** | 6 (1⅓-cup) servings

- 1 cup LAND O.LAKES™ Heavy Whipping Cream
- ½ cup chicken broth
- ¼ cup finely chopped onion
- 2 tablespoons all-purpose flour
- ¼ teaspoon salt
- ¼ teaspoon pepper
- 2 pounds (6 cups) baking potatoes, peeled, thinly sliced
- 1 cup cubed ½-inch deli ham
- 4 ounces (1 cup) LAND O LAKES® Monterey Jack Cheese, shredded
- 4 ounces (1 cup) LAND O LAKES® Cheddar Cheese, shredded
- 1 (9-ounce) package frozen chopped broccoli, thawed, drained

• Heat oven to 375°F. Combine whipping cream, chicken broth, onion, flour, salt and pepper in 2-quart saucepan. Cook over low heat, stirring constantly, until bubbles appear around edges and mixture is thickened (4 to 5 minutes).

• Layer half of potatoes in greased 13×9-inch baking dish or 3-quart casserole. Sprinkle with ham, ½ cup Monterey Jack cheese and ½ cup Cheddar cheese. Cover with remaining potatoes.

• Pour hot cream mixture over potatoes; cover. Bake for 50 to 60 minutes or until potatoes are almost tender when pierced with fork. Uncover; top with broccoli and remaining cheeses. Continue baking for 15 minutes or until potatoes are tender and cheese is melted.

tip:

Baking potatoes are also called russets or Idaho potatoes. They have an elongated shape and thick, brown skin.

Deep-Dish Chicken Pot Pie

Preparation time: **45 minutes** | Baking time: **1 hour** | **6 servings**

Crust

- 2 cups all-purpose flour
- ¼ teaspoon salt
- ⅔ cup cold LAND O LAKES® Butter
- 4 to 6 tablespoons cold water

Filling

- ¼ cup milk
- 1 (10.75-ounce) can condensed cream of chicken soup
- 2 cups cubed 1-inch cooked chicken or turkey
- 4 ounces (1 cup) LAND O LAKES® Cheddar Cheese, shredded
- 1 (16-ounce) package frozen vegetable combination (broccoli, cauliflower, carrots)
- 1½ teaspoons fresh thyme leaves*
- 1 egg, slightly beaten
- 1 teaspoon water

• Heat oven to 375°F. Combine flour and salt in large bowl; cut in butter with pastry blender or fork until mixture resembles coarse crumbs. Mix in enough cold water with fork until flour is moistened. Divide dough in half. Shape each half into a ball; flatten slightly. Wrap 1 ball in plastic food wrap; refrigerate.

• Roll out remaining ball of dough on lightly floured surface into 12-inch circle. Fold into quarters. Place dough into ungreased 9½-inch (deep-dish) pie pan; unfold dough, pressing firmly against bottom and sides. Trim crust to ½ inch from rim of pan; set aside.

• Combine milk and soup in large bowl; mix well. Add all remaining filling ingredients except egg and 1 teaspoon water. Spoon filling into prepared pie crust.

• Roll out refrigerated ball of dough on lightly floured surface into 12-inch circle. Cut 3-inch "X" in center of pastry; cut each pastry triangle in half again. Gently fold dough into quarters. Place dough over filling; unfold. Trim, seal and crimp or flute edge. Fold back the 8 points of pastry in center to form an open circle.

• Combine egg and 1 teaspoon water in small bowl; lightly brush crust with egg mixture. Bake for 60 to 70 minutes or until golden brown. Let stand 10 minutes before serving.

*Substitute ½ teaspoon dried thyme leaves.

Chicken Pesto Bake

Preparation time: **15 minutes** | Baking time: **30 minutes** | 8 (1¼-cup) servings

- 1 (12-ounce) package (4 cups) uncooked dried multi-colored rotini pasta
- 3 cups cubed cooked chicken
- 1 cup milk
- ¼ cup purchased pesto sauce
- 1 (16-ounce) jar Alfredo sauce
- 1 (7-ounce) jar roasted red peppers, drained, chopped
- ⅛ teaspoon pepper
- ½ cup dried bread crumbs
- ½ cup shredded Parmesan cheese
- 2 tablespoons LAND O LAKES® Butter, melted

• Heat oven to 350°F. Cook pasta as directed on package; drain.

• Meanwhile, combine chicken, milk, pesto, Alfredo sauce, red peppers and pepper in large bowl. Stir in cooked pasta. Spread into greased 2-quart baking dish. Cover with aluminum foil. Bake 20 minutes.

• Combine bread crumbs, Parmesan cheese and butter in small bowl. Sprinkle over casserole. Continue baking, uncovered, until edges are bubbly and topping is golden brown (10 to 15 minutes).

tip:
To reduce the calories in this casserole, use light or reduced-fat Alfredo sauce.

tip:
A 12-ounce chicken breast, cooked, equals 3 cups cubed.

tip:
To make ahead, prepare as directed above except shorten pasta cooking time by 2 minutes. Do not top with bread crumb mixture. Do not bake. Cover; refrigerate up to 24 hours. When ready to make, top with bread crumb mixture. Increase first bake time to 30 minutes.

Fiesta Pork Pie

Preparation time: **15 minutes** | Baking time: **35 minutes** | **6 servings**

Filling

- 1 tablespoon LAND O LAKES® Butter
- ⅓ cup chopped onion
- ¾ pound boneless pork loin, cut into bite-sized strips
- ½ teaspoon cornstarch
- 1 (14.5-ounce) can Mexican-style stewed tomatoes
- 1 (15-ounce) can black beans, rinsed, drained
- ½ cup frozen whole kernel corn
- 2 teaspoons chili powder
- 4 ounces (1 cup) LAND O LAKES® Cheddar Cheese, shredded

Crust

- 1 (11½-ounce) container refrigerated cornbread twists

• Heat oven to 375°F. Melt butter in 12-inch skillet until sizzling; add onion. Cook over medium-high heat, stirring occasionally, until onion is softened (2 to 3 minutes). Add pork; cook, stirring occasionally, until no longer pink (3 to 5 minutes). Stir in cornstarch.

• Add tomatoes, beans, corn and chili powder; continue cooking, stirring occasionally, until mixture comes to a boil (3 to 5 minutes). Remove from heat. Stir in cheese. Spoon pork mixture into ungreased 8-inch square baking dish.

• Unroll cornbread dough; separate to form 16 strips. Pinch ends of 2 strips together. Twist strips; pinch other ends together. Repeat with remaining strips. Place 4 twisted strips across pork mixture. Place remaining twisted strips crossways over first strips; cover with aluminum foil. Bake 20 minutes; remove foil. Continue baking for 15 to 20 minutes or until golden brown.

Italian Chicken Cacciatore

Preparation time: **15 minutes** | Cooking time: **46 minutes** | **8 servings**

  2 tablespoons LAND O LAKES® Butter
  1 (3- to 4-pound) package cut-up broiler-fryer chicken, skinned
  2 (14.5-ounce) cans Italian-style diced tomatoes
  1 (4-ounce) can sliced mushrooms, drained
  1 medium onion, cut into eighths
  1 medium green bell pepper, cut into ½-inch pieces
 ½ teaspoon salt
 ¼ teaspoon pepper
  1 (9-ounce) package refrigerated fresh fettuccine, cut in half

• Melt butter in 12-inch skillet until sizzling; add chicken pieces. Cook over medium-high heat, turning once, until browned (10 to 12 minutes).

• Add all remaining ingredients except fettuccine. Cover; continue cooking until chicken is no longer pink (30 to 40 minutes).

• Just before serving, stir in fettuccine. Cover; continue cooking, stirring occasionally, until fettuccine is tender (6 to 9 minutes).

Pesto 'n Shrimp Risotto

Preparation time: **10 minutes** | Cooking time: **27 minutes** | **4 (1-cup) servings**

 2 tablespoons LAND O LAKES® Butter
 1 cup sliced fresh mushrooms
 1 small (¾ cup) leek, thinly sliced*
 1 cup Arborio or short-grain rice
 1 (14-ounce) can chicken broth
 ½ cup hot water
 3 tablespoons prepared pesto sauce
 ½ pound small (36 to 45 count) frozen cooked shrimp, thawed, drained
 1 tablespoon lemon juice

• Melt butter in 2-quart saucepan until sizzling; add mushrooms and leek. Cook over medium-high heat, stirring occasionally, until tender (3 to 5 minutes). Stir in rice; continue cooking until lightly browned (2 to 3 minutes). Stir in chicken broth. Continue cooking until mixture comes to a boil (3 to 5 minutes).

• Reduce heat to medium. Cook, stirring occasionally, until liquid is absorbed (8 to 10 minutes). Stir in hot water. Continue cooking, stirring occasionally, until liquid is absorbed (8 to 10 minutes). Stir in pesto. Stir in shrimp and lemon juice. Cover; continue cooking until shrimp are heated through (3 to 4 minutes).

*Substitute 1 small onion, sliced.

tip:
Run shrimp under cool water to quickly thaw; drain well.

Creamy Alfredo Shrimp Casserole

Preparation time: **20 minutes** | Baking time: **55 minutes** | **4 servings**

 8 ounces (3 cups) uncooked dried farfalle (bow tie) pasta
 1 (10-ounce) container refrigerated Alfredo sauce
 ¾ cup LAND O LAKES™ Fat Free Half & Half or milk
 ¼ cup shredded Parmesan cheese
 ¼ teaspoon coarse ground pepper
 1 (12-ounce) package frozen medium (31 to 35 count) cooked shrimp, thawed, peeled, deveined
 ⅓ cup dried bread crumbs
 2 tablespoons LAND O LAKES® Butter, melted
 ½ teaspoon Italian seasoning*

• Heat oven to 350°F. Cook pasta according to package directions. Drain.

• Combine Alfredo sauce, half & half, Parmesan cheese and pepper in large bowl. Add cooked pasta and shrimp; gently stir to combine.

• Spoon mixture into greased 2-quart casserole. Cover; bake for 40 minutes.

• Toss together bread crumbs, butter and Italian seasoning. Sprinkle bread crumb mixture over pasta mixture. Continue baking, uncovered, for 15 to 20 minutes or until bubbly.

*Substitute ⅛ teaspoon each dried basil leaves, dried marjoram leaves and dried oregano leaves and a dash rubbed sage.

tip:
Properly cooked pasta requires lots of boiling water. Allow about 3 quarts water for each 4 to 8 ounces of dried pasta. Add the pasta, a little at a time, keeping the water boiling. Stir the pasta occasionally during cooking. Drain it when it's tender but still firm.

Pan-Roasted Turkey & Vegetables

Preparation time: **15 minutes** | Baking time: **40 minutes** | **6 servings**

Turkey

¼ cup LAND O LAKES® Butter

½ teaspoon dried thyme leaves

¼ teaspoon salt

¼ teaspoon coarse ground pepper

2 (¾-pound each) turkey tenderloins

Vegetables

3 cups cauliflower florets

2 cups broccoli florets

4 medium carrots, sliced

2 small onions, cut into quarters

• Heat oven to 400°F. Melt butter in small roasting pan until sizzling; stir in thyme, salt and pepper. Add turkey tenderloins. Cook over medium-high heat, turning occasionally, until browned on all sides (8 to 10 minutes).

• Add cauliflower, broccoli, carrots and onions to turkey. Cover; bake for 40 to 45 minutes or until turkey is no longer pink or until meat thermometer reaches 165°F. and vegetables are crisply tender. Serve with pan juices.

Smoked Sausage Rigatoni Bake

Preparation time: **10 minutes** | Baking time: **40 minutes** | **6 (1½-cup) servings**

   8 ounces (3 cups) uncooked dried rigatoni pasta
   1 (14- to 16-ounce) package cooked smoked turkey sausage, cut into ½-inch slices
   1 (14- to 15-ounce) jar pizza sauce*
   ¼ cup LAND O LAKES™ Heavy Whipping Cream**
   1 (2.25-ounce) can (½ cup) sliced ripe olives, drained
   4 ounces (1 cup) LAND O LAKES® Mozzarella Cheese, shredded

• Heat oven to 350°F. Cook pasta according to package directions. Drain.

• Combine all ingredients except cheese in greased 3-quart casserole. Cover; bake for 30 minutes. Uncover; sprinkle with cheese. Continue baking, uncovered, for 10 to 15 minutes or until rigatoni mixture is heated through and cheese is melted.

*Substitute 1½ cups of your favorite flavor of spaghetti sauce.
**Substitute 3 tablespoons milk and 1 tablespoon melted LAND O LAKES® Butter.

tip:
Pasta shapes can be substituted as long as you choose another that is similar in shape and size. Mostaccioli, penne or ziti are great substitutes for rigatoni. Because pasta will continue to cook when used in baked recipes, cook it the minimum amount of time listed on the package.

Asian Crab Cakes with Sesame Sour Cream, p. 116

Mini Mexi Bites *(opposite page)*, p. 121

APPETIZERS

Whether your gathering is a formal occasion, an open house, a backyard barbecue, or just snack time, bite-sized finger foods that provide a burst of flavor are a welcome addition.

Pepper Cheese & Chive Gougère

Preparation time: **15 minutes** | Baking time: **18 minutes** | **42 appetizers**

     1 cup water
     ½ cup LAND O LAKES® Butter
     1 cup all-purpose flour
     ½ teaspoon Italian seasoning*
     ¼ teaspoon garlic salt
     4 eggs
   1½ cups LAND O LAKES® Hot Pepper Jack Cheese, shredded
     2 tablespoons chopped fresh chives

• Heat oven to 400°F. Line baking sheets with parchment paper or lightly spray baking sheets with no-stick cooking spray.

• Combine water and butter in 2-quart saucepan. Cook over medium heat until mixture comes to a boil (5 to 7 minutes). Add flour, Italian seasoning and garlic salt. Stir vigorously until mixture forms a ball. Remove from heat. Beat in eggs, 1 at a time, until smooth. Stir in 1 cup cheese and chives.

• Drop by rounded teaspoonfuls onto parchment-lined baking sheets. Top each with about ½ teaspoon remaining cheese. Bake for 18 to 22 minutes or until puffed and browned. Serve warm.

*Substitute ⅛ teaspoon each dried basil leaves, dried marjoram leaves and dried oregano leaves and a dash rubbed sage.

tip:
Gougère (goo-zhair) is a cheese-flavored cream puff pastry that can be served hot or cold.

tip:
To make ahead and freeze, bake as directed. When completely cooled, place baking sheets in freezer until puffs are frozen. Place frozen puffs in resealable plastic freezer bags or containers; return to freezer. To reheat, place puffs on baking sheet; bake at 350°F. for 8 to 10 minutes or until heated through.

Spicy Skewered Chicken with Peanut Dip

Preparation time: **30 minutes** | Broiling time: 4 **minutes** | **16 appetizers**

Peanut Sauce

¼ cup peanut butter
1 tablespoon chili sauce
1 tablespoon peanut oil or vegetable oil
1 teaspoon finely chopped lemon grass*
½ to ¾ teaspoon crushed red pepper
⅛ teaspoon ground ginger

Dip

¾ cup LAND O LAKES® Sour Cream
3 tablespoons coconut milk or milk

Chicken

1 tablespoon firmly packed brown sugar
2 teaspoons finely chopped lemon grass**
2 teaspoons peanut oil or vegetable oil
1 teaspoon soy sauce
1 pound boneless skinless chicken breasts, cut into 16 (6×½-inch) strips
16 (6- to 8-inch) wooden skewers, soaked in water 30 minutes
1 small cucumber, seeded, cut into 16 chunks, if desired

• Stir together all peanut sauce ingredients in small bowl with wire whisk.

• Stir together 3 tablespoons peanut sauce, sour cream and coconut milk in small bowl. Cover; refrigerate until serving time.

• Heat broiler. Combine remaining peanut sauce, brown sugar, 2 teaspoons lemon grass, 2 teaspoons oil and soy sauce in medium bowl. Add chicken strips; toss to coat. Thread 1 strip chicken onto each wooden skewer.

• Place skewers on broiler pan. Broil 4 to 5 inches from heat, turning once, until chicken is no longer pink (4 to 5 minutes).

• To serve, thread 1 chunk cucumber on each skewer, if desired. Serve warm with dip.

*Substitute 1 teaspoon finely chopped chives and ¼ teaspoon freshly grated lemon peel.
**Substitute 2 teaspoons finely chopped chives and ½ teaspoon freshly grated lemon peel.

tip:
For more peanut butter flavor, add an additional 1 or 2 tablespoons peanut butter to peanut sauce.

California Crab Melt

Preparation time: **20 minutes** | Broiling time: **3 minutes** | **20 appetizers**

  1 (8-ounce) package crabmeat or imitation crabmeat, coarsely chopped
  ½ cup light mayonnaise
  ¼ cup sliced green onions
  6 ounces (1½ cups) LAND O LAKES® Swiss Cheese, shredded
  ½ teaspoon garlic salt
  ¼ teaspoon paprika

20 slices sourdough or French bread baguette

• Heat broiler. Combine all ingredients except bread in medium bowl.

• Place bread slices onto large baking sheet. Broil 5 to 6 inches from heat until toasted (1 to 2 minutes). Turn bread slices over; spread each with about 1 tablespoon crabmeat mixture. Broil 5 to 6 inches from heat until cheese is bubbly (2 to 3 minutes). Serve immediately.

Cheddar Shortbread Bites

Preparation time: **20 minutes** | Baking time: **12 minutes** | **60 appetizers**

Shortbread

- 1 cup all-purpose flour
- ½ cup LAND O LAKES® Butter, softened
- ½ teaspoon salt
  Dash ground red pepper
- 8 ounces (2 cups) LAND O LAKES®
  Sharp Cheddar Cheese, shredded

Topping

- 2 tablespoons poppy seed
- 2 tablespoons sesame seed
- 1 egg white
- 1 tablespoon water

• Combine flour, butter, salt and ground red pepper in medium bowl; beat at medium speed until dough forms. Add cheese; mix until ball forms. Shape dough into 8-inch ball; flatten slightly. Wrap in plastic food wrap; refrigerate 2 hours or overnight.

• Heat oven to 350°F. Roll out dough on lightly floured surface to ¼-inch thickness. (It will be hard to roll at first, but will soften. Press together any cracks that form on edges of dough.) Cut dough with 1½-inch cookie cutters or pizza cutter into desired shapes (squares, triangles, circles). Place onto ungreased baking sheets.

• Combine poppy seed and sesame seed in small bowl. Beat egg white and water in another small bowl. Brush cut-outs with egg white mixture; sprinkle with seed mixture.

• Bake for 12 to 15 minutes or until very lightly browned around edges. Immediately loosen from baking sheets; cool on baking sheets.

tip:

Lining baking sheets with kitchen parchment paper makes shortbread easier to remove and clean-up faster.

tip:

Shortbread can be topped with a variety of other ingredients, such as chili powder, seasoned salt, fennel seed or herbs.

Portabella Pesto Toasts

Preparation time: **15 minutes** | Broiling time: **1 minute** | **12 appetizers**

 ⅓ cup LAND O LAKES® Butter
 1 (6-ounce) package baby portabella mushrooms, cut into ¼-inch slices
 1 teaspoon garlic powder
 12 (¾-inch thick) slices French bread
 ½ cup prepared pesto sauce
 3 ounces (¾ cup) LAND O LAKES® Mozzarella Cheese, shredded

• Heat broiler. Melt 2 tablespoons butter in large skillet until sizzling; add mushrooms and garlic powder. Cook over medium-high heat, stirring occasionally, until tender (about 5 minutes). Remove from heat; set aside.

• Spread 1 side of each bread slice with butter. Place, buttered-side up, onto ungreased baking sheet. Broil 4 to 6 inches from heat until lightly toasted (about 30 seconds). Remove from broiler.

• Turn bread slices over. Spread untoasted sides evenly with pesto, spreading to completely cover bread slices. Top evenly with mushrooms and cheese. Continue broiling until cheese is melted (about 30 seconds). Serve immediately.

tip:
Substitute your favorite fresh mushrooms for the portabella mushrooms.

tip:
Look for refrigerated pesto in the refrigerated pasta section of your supermarket.

Rustic Vegetable Tart

Preparation time: **30 minutes** | Baking time: **21 minutes** | **8 servings**

Pastry

1 cup all-purpose flour
½ cup cold LAND O LAKES® Butter
2 to 3 tablespoons cold water

Filling

1 tablespoon olive oil
⅓ cup chopped sun-dried tomatoes in oil
1 small (1 cup) zucchini, cut into julienne strips
1 small orange or yellow bell pepper, cut into thin strips
1 teaspoon finely chopped fresh garlic
½ cup chopped fresh basil leaves*
⅓ cup chopped pitted kalamata olives
4 ounces (1 cup) crumbled feta cheese
2 tablespoons pine nuts

• Heat oven to 450°F. Place flour in large bowl; cut in butter with pastry blender or fork until mixture resembles coarse crumbs. Mix in enough cold water with fork until flour is moistened. Shape into ball.

• Roll out pastry on lightly floured surface into 12-inch circle. Place into ungreased 9- or 10-inch tart pan with removable bottom or pie pan. Press firmly onto bottom and up sides of pan. Cut away excess pastry; prick all over with fork. Bake for 11 to 14 minutes or until golden brown.

• Meanwhile, heat oil in 10-inch skillet until hot; add tomatoes, zucchini, bell pepper and garlic. Cook over medium-high heat, stirring occasionally, until vegetables are tender and liquid is evaporated (5 to 6 minutes). Stir in basil and olives.

• Spoon tomato mixture evenly into baked pastry shell; sprinkle with cheese and pine nuts. Bake for 10 to 12 minutes or until filling is hot. Let stand 5 minutes before serving. Cut into wedges. Serve warm or cold. Cover; store refrigerated.

*Substitute 2 teaspoons dried basil leaves.

tip:

Portions of this tart can be made ahead of time and assembled and baked before serving. Partially bake the crust as directed and store uncovered at room temperature up to 24 hours. Cook the vegetables as directed in step 3 but do not add the olives and basil. Cover and refrigerate up to 24 hours. Allow vegetables to stand 30 minutes at room temperature before filling crust. Stir in basil and olives. Continue as directed in step 4.

Southwestern Quesadillas

Preparation time: **30 minutes** | Baking time: **10 minutes** | **6 servings**

Filling

- ⅓ cup mayonnaise
- ⅓ cup LAND O LAKES® Sour Cream
- 4 ounces (1 cup) sliced deli chicken breast, cut into small pieces
- 4 ounces (1 cup) LAND O LAKES® Chedarella® Cheese, shredded
- 2 tablespoons sliced green onions
- 2 tablespoons chopped mild green chiles, drained
- ½ teaspoon freshly grated lime peel
- 3 drops hot pepper sauce

Tortillas

- 6 (8-inch) flour tortillas
- 1 tablespoon LAND O LAKES® Butter, melted

  Ground red pepper or chili powder

Toppings

  LAND O LAKES® Sour Cream

  Salsa

- Heat oven to 375°F. Combine all filling ingredients in large bowl.

- Spread about ⅓ cup filling mixture on half of each tortilla; fold other side of tortilla over cheese mixture. Brush both sides of each tortilla with butter; sprinkle top with ground red pepper. Place onto ungreased large baking sheet.

- Bake for 10 to 15 minutes or until heated through.

- To serve, cut each quesadilla into 3 wedges. Serve with sour cream and salsa.

Asian Crab Cakes with Sesame Sour Cream

Preparation time: **30 minutes** | Baking time: **5 minutes** | **42 crab cakes**

Sauce

- ¾ cup LAND O LAKES® Sour Cream
- 1 tablespoon prepared horseradish
- 1½ teaspoons sesame oil
- 1 tablespoon toasted sesame seed

Crab Cakes

- ½ cup sliced green onion
- ⅓ cup LAND O LAKES® Sour Cream or mayonnaise
- 2 teaspoons finely chopped gingerroot
- 1 teaspoon finely chopped garlic
- 2 teaspoons soy sauce
- 1 egg, slightly beaten
- 1 pound lump crabmeat, picked over for shells*
- 2 cups finely crushed saltine crackers
- 3 tablespoons LAND O LAKES® Butter
- 6 tablespoons olive oil

• Heat oven to 400°F. Combine all sauce ingredients in small bowl; mix well; set aside.

• Combine green onion, sour cream, gingerroot, garlic, soy sauce and egg in medium bowl. Stir in crab and 1 cup cracker crumbs until well mixed.

• Shape level tablespoons of mixture into 1½-inch patties; flatten slightly. Place remaining 1 cup crushed crackers in shallow dish. Coat both sides of each patty in crackers.

• Melt 1 tablespoon butter and 2 tablespoons olive oil in 12-inch nonstick skillet over medium heat. Place one-third of crab cakes in pan. Cook, turning once, until golden brown on each side (4 to 6 minutes). Repeat 2 more times with remaining butter, olive oil and crab cakes.

• Place browned cakes onto baking sheets. Bake for 5 to 8 minutes or until heated through. Serve immediately with sour cream sauce.

*Substitute 4 (6-ounce) cans white crab. Drain well to remove excess liquid.

tip:
Patties can be made up to 8 hours ahead. Prepare crab mixture, make patties and coat each in crushed crackers. Place in resealable plastic food container between sheets of waxed paper. Cover tightly; refrigerate. Just before serving, cook and bake crab cakes as directed above.

tip:
Crab cakes may be made ahead and frozen up to 2 weeks. Thaw at room temperature for 20 minutes. To reheat; place crab cakes on baking sheets. Cover with foil; bake at 350°F. for 10 to 12 minutes or until heated through. Serve immediately.

Blue Cheese Bruschetta

Preparation time: **15 minutes** | Baking time: **13 minutes** | **12 appetizers**

  12 (½-inch thick) slices baguette-style French bread
   2 tablespoons LAND O LAKES® Butter, softened
   2 ounces (½ cup) blue cheese crumbles
   1 teaspoon finely chopped fresh chives or green onions
     Dash ground red pepper
  ¼ cup finely chopped red and/or yellow bell pepper*
   1 tablespoon finely chopped fresh parsley

• Heat oven to 400°F. Spread 1 side of bread slices with 1 tablespoon butter. Place onto ungreased baking sheet, buttered-side up. Bake for 8 to 10 minutes or until edges are golden brown. Cool slightly.

• Meanwhile, combine remaining butter, blue cheese, chives and ground red pepper in small bowl; mix well.

• Turn bread slices over. Spread unbuttered sides evenly with blue cheese mixture; sprinkle with bell pepper. Bake for 5 to 6 minutes or until cheese mixture begins to melt. Sprinkle with parsley. Serve warm.

*Substitute ¼ cup finely chopped walnuts.

tip:
For easy entertaining, prepare toasted bread slices and cheese mixture early in the day of your get-together. Store toasted bread slices in a tightly covered container at room temperature and cheese mixture covered in the refrigerator. When ready to prepare appetizers, let cheese mixture come to room temperature for easier spreading.

BLT Focaccia Squares

Preparation time: **40 minutes** | Baking time: **22 minutes** | 32 appetizers

- 1 (1-pound) loaf frozen white bread dough, thawed
- 2 tablespoons mayonnaise
- 2 teaspoons Dijon-style mustard
- ¼ teaspoon freshly ground black pepper
- 4 to 5 (1½ cups) Roma tomatoes, chopped
- ½ pound (about 8 slices) crisply cooked bacon, crumbled
- 6 ounces (1½ cups) LAND O LAKES® Monterey Jack Cheese, shredded
- ⅓ cup sliced green onions
- 1 cup thinly sliced romaine lettuce leaves

• Heat oven to 400°F. Stretch or roll bread dough into greased 15×10×1-inch jelly-roll pan. (If dough is difficult to stretch, cover with plastic food wrap and let rest 10 minutes, then continue stretching to fit into pan.)

• Combine mayonnaise, mustard and pepper in small bowl. Spread evenly over dough. Combine tomatoes, bacon, ¾ cup cheese and green onions in medium bowl; toss lightly. Sprinkle over dough.

• Bake for 20 to 25 minutes or until edges of crust are golden brown. Sprinkle with remaining cheese; continue baking just until cheese is melted (2 to 3 minutes). Immediately sprinkle with lettuce. Cut into squares. Serve warm.

Mini Mexi Bites

Preparation time: **30 minutes** | Baking time: **23 minutes** | **24 appetizers**

  2 eggs
¼ cup milk
  2 tablespoons chopped roasted red pepper
  2 tablespoons sliced green onions
  2 tablespoons chopped fresh cilantro
¼ teaspoon salt
  6 ounces (1½ cups) LAND O LAKES® Hot Pepper Jack Cheese, shredded
  1 (15-ounce) box refrigerated pie crusts, at room temperature

• Heat oven to 350°F. Combine all ingredients except cheese and pie crusts in small bowl. Stir in cheese.

• Spray 24 mini muffin pan cups with no-stick cooking spray. Cut each pie crust into 12 rounds using 2½-inch round cookie cutter. Gently press 1 pie crust round into each muffin cup.

• Evenly pour egg mixture into crust-lined muffin cups. Bake for 23 to 33 minutes or until golden brown.

tip:

If you don't have a cookie cutter, use a 2½-inch round glass and cut around it using a sharp knife.

Savory Snack Mix

Preparation time: **10 minutes** | Baking time: **20 minutes** | **24 (½-cup) servings**

    5 cups corn, rice or wheat cereal squares
    2 cups oyster crackers
    2 cups pretzel sticks, broken in half
 1½ cups sweetened dried cranberries
    1 (9.5-ounce) can (2 cups) salted cashew halves
   ½ cup LAND O LAKES® Butter, melted
    1 (1.2-ounce) package Caesar or Italian dry salad dressing mix

• Heat oven to 300°F. Combine all ingredients except butter and salad dressing mix in ungreased large roasting pan.

• Combine butter and salad dressing mix in small bowl. Pour over cereal mixture; toss to coat.

• Bake for 20 to 30 minutes, stirring twice, until lightly browned. Cool completely. Store in container with tight-fitting lid.

tip:
Snack may be baked in 2 (13×9-inch) baking pans or 2 (15×10×1-inch) jelly-roll pans.

Easy Chili Bean Dip

Preparation time: **5 minutes** | Cooking time: **8 minutes** | 2½ cups

  ½ cup medium or hot picante sauce
  8 ounces (2 cups) LAND O LAKES® Deli American Cheese, shredded
  1 (15-ounce) can black beans, rinsed, drained
  1 (4-ounce) can mild or hot chopped green chiles, drained

    Tortilla chips

• Combine all ingredients except tortilla chips in 2-quart saucepan. Cook over low heat, stirring constantly, until cheese is melted (8 to 10 minutes).

• Serve warm with tortilla chips.

tip:
A small electric slow cooker makes a great serving container and keeps the dip warm. Keep it set on Low heat setting.

Buttermilk Herb Fried Chicken, p. 130

Asian Pork Noodle Bowl *(opposite page)*, p. 138

ENTRÉES

Once you try these appetizing main dishes, you'll want to serve them again and again. So whether it's for a special occasion or an everyday supper, gather everyone around the table to share a delicious meal.

Oven-Baked Chicken

Preparation time: **15 minutes** | Baking time: **45 minutes** | **8 servings**

> 1 cup dried bread crumbs
> ⅓ cup grated Parmesan cheese
> 2 tablespoons finely chopped parsley
> ½ teaspoon pepper
> ¼ teaspoon salt
> ½ cup LAND O LAKES® Butter, melted
> 2 teaspoons finely chopped fresh garlic
> 1 (3- to 3½-pound) cut-up broiler-fryer chicken

• Heat oven to 375°F. Combine bread crumbs, Parmesan cheese, parsley, pepper and salt in shallow bowl; set aside.

• Combine butter and garlic in 9-inch pie pan. Dip each chicken piece, 1 at a time, into butter mixture; place into bread crumb mixture, turning to coat evenly. Place chicken pieces onto ungreased 15×10×1-inch baking pan, skin-side up. Drizzle with any remaining butter.

• Bake for 45 to 55 minutes or until chicken is lightly browned and juices run clear when pierced with fork.

tip:
Adding herbs to a recipe can change the way it tastes. For flavor variations, try mixing ½ teaspoon dried herbs, such as rosemary or sage, into the melted butter mixture.

tip:
The skin can be removed from the chicken pieces before coating, if desired.

Shrimp Diablo

Preparation time: **10 minutes** | Cooking time: **12 minutes** | **4 (1¼-cup) servings**

2	tablespoons LAND O LAKES® Butter
3	medium (3 cups) zucchini, cut into ½-inch slices
1	medium (½ cup) onion, sliced
1	teaspoon finely chopped fresh garlic
1	(14.5-ounce) can diced tomatoes with Italian herbs
1	(12-ounce) package frozen medium (31 to 35 count) cooked shrimp, thawed, drained
¼	teaspoon ground red pepper
4	cups hot cooked rice or couscous

• Melt butter in 10-inch skillet until sizzling; add zucchini, onion and garlic. Cook over medium-high heat, stirring occasionally, until vegetables are crisply tender (3 to 4 minutes).

• Stir in diced tomatoes, shrimp and ground red pepper. Continue cooking until mixture comes to a full boil (3 to 4 minutes). Reduce heat to medium. Cover; cook, stirring occasionally, until shrimp are heated through (6 to 8 minutes). Serve over rice.

tip:

To prevent garlic cloves from rolling around on the cutting board, smash them flat first with the wide end of a large knife, such as a French or chef's knife, then begin to chop.

Pork Chops with Caramelized Onions

Preparation time: **5 minutes** | Cooking time: **22 minutes** | **4 servings**

    ¼ cup LAND O LAKES® Butter
    4 (½-inch thick) pork chops
    ½ teaspoon salt
    ½ teaspoon coarse ground pepper
    3 medium onions, thinly sliced
    ¼ teaspoon dried rosemary*
    2 teaspoons finely chopped fresh garlic

• Melt butter in 10-inch skillet until sizzling; add pork chops. Cook over medium-high heat, turning once, until browned (8 to 10 minutes). Season with salt and pepper. Remove chops to serving platter. Keep warm.

• Place onions in skillet with pan juices; sprinkle with rosemary. Cook over medium heat, stirring occasionally, until onions are caramelized (8 to 10 minutes). Stir in garlic; continue cooking until garlic is softened (2 to 3 minutes).

• Return chops to pan; continue cooking until pork is no longer pink (4 to 5 minutes).

*Substitute 1 teaspoon chopped fresh rosemary.

Buttermilk Herb Fried Chicken

Preparation time: **10 minutes** | Cooking time: **20 minutes** | **4 servings**

Coating

½ cup all-purpose flour

1 tablespoon chopped fresh parsley*

1 tablespoon fresh thyme leaves**

1 teaspoon salt

½ teaspoon garlic powder

¼ teaspoon pepper

Chicken

1 (20-ounce) package boneless skinless chicken breast halves

⅓ cup buttermilk***

⅓ cup LAND O LAKES® Butter

• Combine all coating ingredients in 9-inch pie pan. Dip chicken breasts in buttermilk, then in coating mixture.

• Melt butter in 12-inch skillet until sizzling; add chicken. Cook over medium-high heat, turning occasionally, until golden brown and fork tender (20 to 25 minutes).

*Substitute 1 teaspoon dried parsley flakes.

**Substitute 1 teaspoon dried thyme leaves.

***Substitute 1 teaspoon vinegar or lemon juice plus enough milk to equal ⅓ cup. Let stand 10 minutes.

tip:
If chicken breasts are too thick, pound them to ½-inch thickness using a meat mallet.

tip:
If chicken breasts are browning too quickly, reduce heat to medium.

Old-Fashioned Pot Roast

Preparation time: **30 minutes** | Baking time: **2 hours** | **8 servings**

Beef

- 1 tablespoon LAND O LAKES® Butter
- 1 (2½- to 3-pound) boneless beef chuck roast (up to 2 inches thick)

Seasoning

- 1 cup water
- 2 teaspoons dried basil leaves*
- 1 teaspoon instant beef bouillon granules
- 3 bay leaves
- ¾ teaspoon salt
- ½ teaspoon pepper

Vegetables

- 8 medium carrots, cut into 3-inch pieces
- 6 medium potatoes, peeled, cut into quarters
- 4 small onions, cut into quarters

Gravy

- Beef broth, if necessary**
- ¼ cup all-purpose flour
- ½ cup cold water

• Heat oven to 325°F. Melt butter in 6-quart ovenproof saucepan until sizzling; add beef roast. Cook over medium-high heat, turning once, until browned (7 to 9 minutes). Drain off fat.

• Combine all seasoning ingredients in small bowl; pour over roast. Add vegetables. Cover; bake for 2 to 2¼ hours or until roast is fork tender. Remove bay leaves. Remove roast and vegetables to serving platter; keep warm.

• Skim fat from pan juices. Measure 1½ cups pan juices, adding beef broth if necessary, return to saucepan.

• Combine flour and cold water in small bowl with wire whisk until smooth; stir into pan juices. Cook over medium heat, stirring constantly with wire whisk, until mixture comes to a full boil (2 to 3 minutes). Boil 1 minute. Serve gravy with roast and vegetables.

*Substitute 2 tablespoons chopped fresh basil leaves.

**To make beef broth, mix 1 cup hot water and 1 teaspoon instant beef bouillon granules.

Spiced Brown Sugar Salmon with Peach-Kiwi Salsa

Preparation time: **15 minutes** | Grilling time: **15 minutes** | **6 servings**

Salsa

- 2 fresh peaches (1 cup), peeled, pitted, coarsely chopped
- 1 kiwifruit, peeled, coarsely chopped
- 2 tablespoons thinly sliced green onions
- 2 tablespoons chopped parsley
- 1 tablespoon lime juice
- ¼ teaspoon crushed red pepper

Glaze

- ¼ cup LAND O LAKES® Butter, melted
- ¼ cup firmly packed brown sugar
- ¾ teaspoon ground cinnamon
- ½ teaspoon salt
- ¼ teaspoon ground cumin
- ¼ teaspoon ground nutmeg
- ¼ teaspoon crushed red pepper

Salmon

- 1 (1½-pound) salmon fillet

• Combine all salsa ingredients in small bowl. Cover; refrigerate at least 1 hour.

• Heat gas grill on medium or charcoal grill until coals are ash white.

• Meanwhile, combine all glaze ingredients in small bowl. Place salmon onto grill, skin-side down. Brush salmon with glaze. Close lid; grill 6 minutes. Brush salmon with remaining glaze. Continue grilling until fish flakes with fork (9 to 10 minutes). Serve with salsa.

tip:
Frozen peaches may be used in place of the fresh peaches. Thaw frozen sliced peaches and chop 1 cup.

oven directions:
Heat oven to 425°F. Place salmon onto aluminum foil-lined 15×10×1-inch baking pan. Brush with glaze. Bake 6 minutes; brush with remaining glaze. Continue baking until fish flakes with fork (10 to 12 minutes).

Easy Chicken Marsala

Preparation time: **10 minutes** | Cooking time: **10 minutes** | **4 servings**

¼ cup all-purpose flour
½ teaspoon salt
¼ teaspoon pepper
4 tablespoons LAND O LAKES® Butter
1 (16-ounce) package boneless skinless chicken breast tenders
1 teaspoon finely chopped fresh garlic
⅔ cup dry Marsala wine or chicken broth
1 (8-ounce) package sliced mushrooms

Hot cooked regular or spinach fettuccine, if desired
Chopped fresh parsley

• Combine flour, salt and pepper in large resealable plastic food storage bag. Melt 2 tablespoons butter in pie pan or shallow bowl. Dip chicken in melted butter; place into bag. Seal bag tightly; shake to coat chicken.

• Melt 2 tablespoons butter in 12-inch skillet until sizzling; add chicken and garlic. Cook over medium-high heat until chicken is browned, turning once (6 to 8 minutes). Add wine and mushrooms. Continue cooking until chicken is no longer pink and sauce is slightly thickened (4 to 6 minutes).

• Serve over fettuccine, if desired. Sprinkle with parsley.

tip:

A Sicilian import, Marsala is Italy's most famous wine. The flavor is very rich and slightly smoky. Dry Marsala is often used in savory cooking whereas the sweet variety finds its way into desserts. In this particular recipe, a dry sherry could be substituted.

Asian Pork Noodle Bowl

Preparation time: **10 minutes** | Cooking time: **9 minutes** | 4 (1½-cup) servings

    4 cups water
    2 (3-ounce) packages oriental flavored ramen noodle soup
    2 tablespoons LAND O LAKES® Butter, melted
    1 teaspoon freshly grated gingerroot
    1 tablespoon LAND O LAKES® Butter
    1 (16-ounce) package fresh or frozen broccoli stir-fry vegetables
    1 cup cubed cooked pork tenderloin

• Bring water to a boil in 4-quart saucepan. Add noodles; reserve spice packets. Cook over medium heat 3 minutes. Drain.

• Meanwhile, combine 2 tablespoons melted butter and gingerroot in small bowl; mix well. Pour ginger butter over cooked noodles; toss to coat. Keep warm.

• Melt 1 tablespoon butter in 10-inch skillet until sizzling; add vegetables. Cook over medium-high heat 2 minutes. Add pork. Cover, continue cooking until vegetables are crisply tender (4 to 5 minutes). Stir in reserved spice packets. Serve pork mixture over noodles.

tip:
Make this into a fun dinner by serving this entrée in deep bowls with chopsticks. For dessert, pass out purchased fortune cookies.

Crunchy Cheese-Stuffed Chicken

Preparation time: **15 minutes** | Baking time: **20 minutes** | **4 servings**

    1 (8-ounce) package LAND O LAKES® Cheddar Cheese
    4 (4-ounce) boneless skinless chicken breast halves
  ½ cup cornflake crumbs
    1 teaspoon seasoning salt*
    1 egg, beaten

• Heat oven to 400°F. Cut 4 (2×1×½-inch) strips from cheese; set aside. Shred ¼ cup cheese from remaining cheese; set aside. Save remainder for another use.

• Cut a 3-inch slit in each chicken breast half to form pocket. Insert 1 strip cheese into each pocket. Secure each pocket with several toothpicks.

• Combine crumbs, ¼ cup shredded cheese and seasoning salt in pie pan or shallow bowl. Place beaten egg in another pie pan or shallow bowl; dip chicken in egg. Lightly press both sides of chicken into crumb mixture to coat.

• Place chicken onto greased baking sheet. Bake for 20 to 25 minutes or until chicken is no longer pink.

*Substitute 1 teaspoon garlic salt.

Turkey Tenderloins with Berry Chutney

Preparation time: **10 minutes** | Cooking time: **19 minutes** | **5 servings**

Turkey

- 2 tablespoons LAND O LAKES® Butter
- 2 teaspoons finely chopped fresh garlic
- 2 (about 10 ounces each) turkey breast tenderloins

Chutney

- ¾ cup whole-berry cranberry sauce
- ¼ cup chopped fresh cilantro
- 2 green onions, sliced
- 1 jalapeño pepper, seeded, chopped
- ¼ teaspoon ground cumin

• Melt butter in 10-inch skillet until sizzling; add garlic. Cook over medium heat, stirring occasionally, 1 minute. Add turkey tenderloins; continue cooking, turning once, until turkey is lightly browned on both sides (5 to 7 minutes). Reduce heat to low. Cover; cook, turning tenderloins over once, until turkey is no longer pink (12 to 14 minutes) or until meat thermometer reaches 165°F.

• Meanwhile, combine all chutney ingredients in medium bowl. Remove turkey from skillet; keep warm. Add chutney to skillet. Cook over medium-high heat until mixture just comes to a boil (2 to 3 minutes). Serve turkey with chutney.

tip:

For milder jalapeño flavor, remove seeds and discard before finely chopping. Be careful when cutting as the seeds and juice can be irritating to sensitive skin. When preparing several peppers, rubber gloves are advised.

Peppered Tenderloin with Mustard Sauce

Preparation time: **15 minutes** | Grilling time: **15 minutes** | **4 servings**

Steaks

  2 tablespoons cracked pepper
  4 (1½-inch thick) beef tenderloin steaks

Sauce

  ½ cup beef broth
  1 teaspoon finely chopped fresh garlic
  1 teaspoon dry sherry or Worcestershire sauce
  ⅓ cup LAND O LAKES® Sour Cream
  ½ teaspoon Dijon-style mustard

    Cracked pepper, if desired

• Heat gas grill on medium or charcoal grill until coals are ash white.

• Press cracked pepper onto both sides of steaks. Place steaks onto grill. Grill, turning once, until internal temperature reaches 145°F. (medium-rare) or until desired doneness (15 to 20 minutes).

• Meanwhile, combine beef broth, garlic and sherry in small saucepan. Cook over medium heat until mixture comes to a boil (5 to 7 minutes). Continue boiling for 5 minutes. Stir in sour cream and mustard with wire whisk. Continue cooking until heated through (1 minute).

• Serve sauce over grilled steaks. Sprinkle with additional cracked pepper, if desired.

Make-Ahead Ranch Mashed Potatoes, p. 148

Strawberry Salad with Poppy Seed Dressing *(opposite page)*, p. 153

SALADS
AND SIDES

What meal is complete without a serving of greens or vegetables?
Start with a crisp, delicious salad, then make sure there's room next
to the entrée for a savory side.

Grilled Sweet Potato Salad

Preparation time: **20 minutes** | Grilling time: **15 minutes** | **6 (½-cup) servings**

- 1 pound (about 3 small) orange sweet potatoes, peeled, cut into 1-inch pieces
- 1 small onion, cut into thin wedges
- 1 small (½ cup) red bell pepper, coarsely chopped
- 2 tablespoons LAND O LAKES® Butter, softened
- ½ teaspoon salt
- ¼ teaspoon pepper
- 1 tablespoon balsamic vinegar
- 2 tablespoons fully cooked real bacon bits*

• Heat gas grill on medium or charcoal grill until coals are ash white. Place sweet potatoes, onion and red bell pepper onto 12-inch length of heavy-duty aluminum foil. Dot top of vegetables with small pieces of softened butter. Top with another 12-inch length of foil. Seal edges of foil by folding over twice.

• Place aluminum foil packet onto grill. Grill, turning once, until potatoes are tender (15 to 20 minutes).

• Carefully open packet; spoon vegetables into serving bowl. Add all remaining ingredients; gently toss to coat. Serve warm or at room temperature.

*Substitute 2 slices bacon, cooked, crumbled.

tip:

Sweet potatoes are found in 2 varieties, a pale-skinned variety and a darker-skinned variety sometimes incorrectly called yams. Pale sweet potatoes have a thin yellow skin and pale yellow flesh. They are not sweet and moist like the darker orange-skinned variety, which has orange flesh.

Make-Ahead Ranch Mashed Potatoes

Preparation time: **10 minutes** | Cooking time: **15 minutes** | Baking time: **40 minutes** | **6 servings**

> 2 pounds (4 cups) peeled potatoes, cut into 1-inch pieces
> ⅓ cup water
> ½ teaspoon salt
> 1 cup milk
> ⅓ cup LAND O LAKES® Sour Cream
> 1½ teaspoons dry ranch salad dressing mix
> 2 tablespoons LAND O LAKES® Butter

• Combine potatoes, water and salt in 2-quart saucepan. Cook over high heat until water comes to a boil. Reduce heat to low. Cover; cook until potatoes are fork tender (15 to 20 minutes). Drain.

• Mash potatoes with potato masher or electric mixer, gradually adding ⅔ cup milk. Stir in sour cream and dressing mix.

• Spread potatoes evenly into ungreased 1½-quart casserole. Pour remaining milk over potatoes. (DO NOT MIX.) Dot with butter. Cover; refrigerate 4 hours or overnight.

• Heat oven to 400°F. Bake uncovered for 20 minutes. Stir; continue baking for 20 to 30 minutes or until heated through.

tip:

For faster heating, place potatoes in microwave-safe casserole. To heat, microwave, covered, on HIGH (100% power), stirring 2 or 3 times, or until heated through (15 to 18 minutes).

variation:

To prepare 12 servings, double all ingredients except use 1¼ cups milk. Cook potatoes as directed above. Mash potatoes with potato masher or electric mixer, gradually adding 1 cup milk. Stir in sour cream and dressing mix. Spread potatoes evenly into ungreased 3-quart casserole. Pour remaining milk over potatoes. Continue as directed above.

Broccoli Peanut Toss

Preparation time: **15 minutes** | **4 (1-cup) servings**

Salad

3½ cups broccoli florets, coarsely chopped

¼ cup raisins

¼ cup roasted salted peanuts

¼ cup finely chopped red onion

2 ounces (½ cup) LAND O LAKES®
Cheddar Cheese, cut into ½-inch
cubes

Dressing

¼ cup mayonnaise

1 tablespoon sugar

1 tablespoon red wine vinegar

• Place all salad ingredients in medium bowl; toss to combine.

• Combine all dressing ingredients in small bowl. Pour over salad; toss to coat. Serve
immediately or refrigerate until serving time.

<u>variation:</u>

Broccoli Cauliflower Toss: Substitute cauliflower florets for half of the broccoli.

California Chop Chop Salad

Preparation time: **15 minutes** | **4 servings**

Salad

¾ cup canned garbanzo beans, drained

½ cup small pitted black olives

1 medium (1 cup) avocado, peeled, pitted, coarsely chopped

1 medium (1 cup) tomato, chopped

1 (6-ounce) jar marinated artichoke hearts, drained, chopped, reserve marinade

3 ounces (¾ cup) LAND O LAKES® Cheddar Cheese, cut into ½-inch cubes

Dressing

¼ cup prepared balsamic vinaigrette*

Lettuce leaves

• Place all salad ingredients in large bowl except reserved marinade.

• Combine ¼ cup reserved marinade and balsamic vinaigrette in small bowl. Pour over salad; toss to coat.

• To serve, place lettuce leaves on serving plate; top with salad mixture.

*Substitute your favorite prepared vinaigrette.

Italian Grilled Corn

Preparation time: **15 minutes** | Grilling time: **15 minutes** | **12 servings**

Spread

¾ cup LAND O LAKES® Butter, softened

2 tablespoons finely chopped red bell pepper

1 teaspoon Italian seasoning*

1 teaspoon salt

½ teaspoon garlic powder

Corn

12 ears fresh corn, husked**

12 (12×18-inch) pieces heavy-duty aluminum foil

• Heat gas grill on medium or charcoal grill until coals are ash white. Combine all spread ingredients in small bowl; mix well.

• Spread 1 tablespoon butter mixture evenly over each ear of corn. Wrap each in aluminum foil, tightly sealing tops and sides. Place packets onto grill. Close lid; grill, turning after half the time, for 15 to 20 minutes or until tender. Serve hot in foil.

oven directions:

Heat oven to 425°F. Prepare corn as directed above. Wrap each ear of corn in aluminum foil, tightly sealing tops and sides. Bake for 20 to 30 minutes or until tender. Serve hot in foil.

*Substitute ¼ teaspoon each dried basil leaves, dried marjoram leaves and dried oregano leaves and ⅛ teaspoon rubbed sage.

**Substitute 12 ears frozen corn on the cob, thawed.

tip:

Prepare spread as directed above. Cook corn as desired. Serve spread on hot corn.

Strawberry Salad with Poppy Seed Dressing

Preparation time: **10 minutes** | Cooking time: **5 minutes** | **6 servings**

Dressing

½ cup LAND O LAKES® Sour Cream
1 tablespoon sugar
2 to 3 tablespoons milk
1 tablespoon orange juice
1 teaspoon freshly grated orange peel
1 teaspoon poppy seed

Pecans

¼ cup coarsely chopped pecans
2 tablespoons sugar

Salad

3 cups torn lettuce
3 cups baby spinach leaves or packaged fresh spinach, torn in bite-sized pieces
2 cups sliced fresh strawberries

• Stir together all dressing ingredients in medium bowl. Refrigerate at least 30 minutes.

• Meanwhile, combine pecans and sugar in 8-inch skillet. Cook over medium heat, stirring constantly, until sugar is melted and pecans are coated and lightly browned (5 to 8 minutes). Spread onto waxed paper-lined baking sheet. Cool completely.

• Just before serving, toss together pecans and all remaining salad ingredients in large bowl. Serve with dressing.

Browned Butter Potatoes

Preparation time: **10 minutes** | Cooking time: **28 minutes** | **8 servings**

 2 pounds small red, white or Yukon Gold potatoes, cut into wedges
 4 cups water
 1 tablespoon beef bouillon granules or beef concentrate
 ¼ cup LAND O LAKES® Butter
 1 tablespoon finely chopped fresh parsley
 ½ teaspoon salt

• Place potatoes, water and bouillon in 4-quart saucepan or Dutch oven. Cover; cook over medium-high heat until mixture comes to a boil (6 to 8 minutes). Reduce heat to low. Cover; cook until potatoes are tender (20 to 22 minutes). Drain.

• Melt butter in 1-quart saucepan over medium heat. Cook, stirring constantly, until butter foams and just starts to turn a delicate golden color (2 to 3 minutes). Stir in parsley and salt. Pour immediately over potatoes; gently stir to coat.

Panzanella

Preparation time: **15 minutes** | Grilling time: **2 minutes** | **5 servings**

- 3 tablespoons LAND O LAKES® Butter, softened
- 1 tablespoon chopped fresh garlic
- 4 (½- to ¾-inch) slices Italian or Vienna bread
- 1 (10-ounce) package romaine salad greens
- 2 cups small broccoli florets
- 1½ cups halved cherry tomatoes
- 4 ounces (1 cup) LAND O LAKES® Mozzarella Cheese, cut into ½-inch cubes
- ¼ cup pitted ripe olives
- ⅔ cup Italian salad dressing

• Heat gas grill to medium or charcoal grill until coals are ash white.

• Combine butter and garlic in small bowl. Spread butter mixture over both sides of bread. Grill, turning once, until toasted (2 to 3 minutes). Cut into 1-inch pieces.

• Place romaine lettuce in salad bowl. Add broccoli, tomatoes, cheese and olives; toss lightly. Add dressing; toss until well coated. Add prepared bread cubes; toss lightly.

tip:

The bread can be grilled up to 4 hours ahead. Cut into pieces; store in loosely covered container.

Almond, Blue Cheese & Cranberry Salad

Preparation time: **25 minutes** | Cooking time: **4 minutes** | **16 (1-cup) servings**

Dressing

- ¼ cup olive oil
- 2 tablespoons sugar
- ½ teaspoon salt
- ⅛ teaspoon pepper
- ¼ cup tarragon white wine vinegar or white wine vinegar
- ½ teaspoon poppy seed

Almonds

- 1 tablespoon LAND O LAKES® Butter
- ½ cup slivered almonds
- 3 tablespoons sugar

Salad

- 2 (10-ounce) bags European salad blend or your favorite salad blend
- 1 medium (1 cup) yellow bell pepper, cut into 1-inch pieces
- ½ cup sliced green onions
- ½ cup sweetened dried cranberries or cherries
- 4 ounces (½ cup) crumbled blue cheese or feta cheese

• Combine all dressing ingredients in jar or small container with tight-fitting lid; shake well to mix. Refrigerate.

• Melt butter in 10-inch skillet over medium heat until sizzling; add almonds and 2 tablespoons sugar. Continue cooking, stirring constantly, until sugar melts and nuts are golden brown (4 to 5 minutes). Remove from heat; sprinkle with remaining 1 tablespoon sugar. Quickly spread onto waxed paper-lined baking sheet; cool completely.

• Just before serving, toss together all salad ingredients, caramelized almonds and dressing in 5- to 6-quart bowl. Serve immediately.

tip:

This salad is very versatile. Try substituting your favorite vegetables, dried fruits and nuts, such as snap peas, red onion, dried apricots, dried or fresh blueberries, pecans, etc. For a smaller salad, simply cut recipe in half.

Calico Coleslaw

Preparation time: **15 minutes** | 6 (⅔-cup) servings

    2 cups cauliflower florets
    2 cups coleslaw mix
    ½ cup (1 medium) shredded carrot
    ¼ cup chopped red onion
    4 ounces (1 cup) LAND O LAKES® Cheddar Cheese, shredded
    5 slices crisply cooked bacon, crumbled, reserve 1 tablespoon
    1 (8-ounce) bottle cucumber or coleslaw salad dressing

• Combine all ingredients except reserved bacon in large salad bowl; toss until well coated. Cover; refrigerate at least 4 hours.

• Just before serving, sprinkle with reserved bacon.

Spring Greens with Toasted Cheese

Preparation time: **20 minutes** | **6 servings**

- ½ cup Italian vinaigrette or honey mustard dressing
- ½ cup dried bread crumbs
- ⅛ teaspoon garlic salt
- 1 (8-ounce) package LAND O LAKES® Monterey Jack, Chedarella® or Co-Jack® Cheese, cut into 18 (¾-inch) cubes
- 7 cups mixed baby salad greens
- 1 cup fresh whole herb leaves (such as parsley, basil, mint or cilantro)
- ¾ cup small cherry tomatoes

• Heat oven to 400°F. Line baking sheet with aluminum foil.

• Place ¼ cup dressing in shallow bowl. Combine bread crumbs and garlic salt in another shallow bowl. Dip each piece of cheese into dressing; shake off excess dressing. Coat with bread crumbs. Place cheese onto prepared baking sheet. Bake for 3 to 4 minutes or just until soft. (DO NOT OVERBAKE.)

• Arrange salad greens, herbs and tomatoes on 6 individual salad plates. Drizzle with remaining dressing. Place 3 cubes toasted cheese on each salad. Serve immediately.

tip:
_____
The crumb-coated cheese cubes can be made well ahead of time. Refrigerate, covered, on baking sheet or in a covered container. Bake just before serving.

Chocolate Truffle Toffee Cheesecake, p. 178

Mandarin Marmalade Cream Cake *(opposite page)*, p. 170

CAKES AND CHEESECAKES

Special occasions call for rich, decadent desserts. Whether it's a creamy cheesecake or a mouthwatering layer cake, your friends and family will make room for the final course.

Chocolate Raspberry Pudding Cake

Preparation time: **20 minutes** | Baking time: **30 minutes** | **9 servings**

- 1 cup all-purpose flour
- ¾ cup sugar
- ¼ cup unsweetened cocoa
- 1 tablespoon baking powder
- ½ teaspoon salt
- ½ cup milk
- 3 tablespoons LAND O LAKES® Butter, melted
- 1 teaspoon vanilla
- 1 (10-ounce) package frozen raspberries in syrup, thawed
- 1 cup hot water
- ⅓ cup chocolate-flavored syrup

  Powdered sugar, if desired
  Fresh raspberries, if desired

• Heat oven to 350°F. Place flour, sugar, cocoa, baking powder and salt in greased 8- or 9-inch square baking pan; stir with fork to combine. Stir in milk, butter and vanilla until well mixed. Stir in raspberries.

• Combine hot water and chocolate syrup in small bowl. Pour evenly over batter. Bake for 30 to 35 minutes or until center is set and edges are pulled away from sides of pan. Let stand 25 minutes. Sprinkle with powdered sugar and garnish with fresh raspberries, if desired. Serve warm.

Double Chocolate Coconut Cake

Preparation time: **20 minutes** | Baking time: **1 hour 10 minutes** | **12 servings**

> 1 cup LAND O LAKES® Butter
> ⅔ cup chocolate-flavored syrup
> 1 (7-ounce) milk chocolate bar, broken into pieces
> 2¼ cups all-purpose flour
> 1 cup sugar
> 1 cup sweetened flaked coconut
> 1 cup milk
> 4 eggs
> 1 tablespoon lemon juice
> 1 tablespoon vanilla
> ½ teaspoon baking soda
>
> Powdered sugar, if desired

• Heat oven to 325°F. Place butter, chocolate syrup and chocolate bar pieces in heavy 2-quart saucepan. Cook over low heat, stirring occasionally, until melted (4 to 5 minutes).

• Beat melted chocolate mixture and all remaining ingredients except powdered sugar in large bowl at medium speed, scraping bowl often, until well mixed.

• Pour batter into greased 12-cup Bundt® or 10-inch angel food cake (tube) pan. Bake for 70 to 80 minutes or until toothpick inserted in center comes out clean. Cool upright in pan 15 minutes. Invert cake onto cooling rack; cool completely. Sprinkle with powdered sugar, if desired.

German Chocolate Cake

Preparation time: **25 minutes** | Baking time: **33 minutes** | **12 servings**

Frosting

3 eggs
1½ cups firmly packed brown sugar
¾ cup LAND O LAKES™ Half & Half
½ cup LAND O LAKES® Butter
1½ cups sweetened flaked coconut
1 cup chopped pecans
2 teaspoons vanilla

Cake

1 (4-ounce) package sweet baking
   chocolate
½ cup water
1 cup sugar
½ cup LAND O LAKES® Butter, softened
2 eggs
1 teaspoon vanilla
1½ cups all-purpose flour
1 teaspoon baking soda
½ teaspoon salt
1 cup buttermilk*

• Slightly beat 3 eggs in 2-quart saucepan with wire whisk. Stir in brown sugar, half & half and ½ cup butter. Cook over medium heat, stirring constantly, until mixture comes to a boil and is thickened (10 to 15 minutes). Remove from heat. Stir in coconut, pecans and 2 teaspoons vanilla. Cool completely (at least 1 hour).

• Meanwhile, heat oven to 350°F. Grease and lightly flour 2 (8- or 9-inch) round cake pans; set aside.

• Combine chocolate and water in 1-quart saucepan. Cook over low heat, stirring occasionally, until chocolate is melted (6 to 7 minutes). Cool 10 minutes.

• Place sugar and ½ cup butter in large bowl. Beat at medium speed, scraping bowl often, until creamy. Add 2 eggs and 1 teaspoon vanilla; continue beating until well mixed. Add chocolate mixture; continue beating until well mixed. Add flour, baking soda and salt alternately with buttermilk, beating well after each addition.

• Pour batter into prepared pans. Bake for 33 to 40 minutes or until toothpick inserted in center comes out clean. Cool 15 minutes. Remove from pans. Cool completely.

• Spread frosting over top of each cake; stack layers. Frost sides of cake, if desired.

*Substitute 1 tablespoon vinegar or lemon juice plus enough milk to equal 1 cup. Let stand 10 minutes.

tip:
This cake can also be baked in a greased 13×9-inch baking pan. Bake for 33 to 40 minutes or until toothpick inserted in center comes out clean.

Mandarin Marmalade Cream Cake

Preparation time: **25 minutes** | Baking time: **28 minutes** | **15 servings**

Cake

- 1 (18.25-ounce) package white cake mix
- 1 (11-ounce) can mandarin orange segments, undrained
- ¼ cup water
- 6 tablespoons LAND O LAKES® Butter, melted, cooled slightly
- 2 eggs

Topping

- 1 cup LAND O LAKES™ Heavy Whipping Cream
- 2 tablespoons powdered sugar
- 1 (12-ounce) jar (1 cup) orange marmalade, divided
- 1 (11-ounce) can mandarin orange segments, well-drained, if desired

• Heat oven to 350°F. Combine all cake ingredients in large bowl. Beat at low speed 30 seconds. Increase speed to medium; beat, scraping bowl often, until well mixed (2 minutes).

• Pour batter into greased 13×9-inch baking pan. Bake for 28 to 33 minutes or until toothpick inserted in center comes out clean. Cool completely.

• Beat whipping cream in chilled small bowl at high speed, scraping bowl often, until soft peaks form. Continue beating, gradually adding powdered sugar, until stiff peaks form. (DO NOT OVERBEAT.) Gently stir in ¼ cup marmalade.

• Spread cooled cake evenly with remaining ¾ cup marmalade. Spread whipped cream mixture over marmalade. Garnish with mandarin orange segments, if desired. Store refrigerated.

Peanut Butter Chocolate Chip Cheesecake

Preparation time: **25 minutes** | Baking time: **1 hour 10 minutes** | **12 servings**

Crust

1½ cups (15 cookies) chocolate sandwich cookie crumbs

3 tablespoons LAND O LAKES® Butter, melted

Filling

½ cup LAND O LAKES® Sour Cream

3 (8-ounce) packages cream cheese, softened

3 eggs

1 cup sugar

¾ cup creamy peanut butter

1 tablespoon cornstarch

1 cup real semi-sweet chocolate chips

LAND O LAKES™ Heavy Whipping Cream, whipped, sweetened, if desired

Chocolate sandwich cookie crumbs, if desired

• Heat oven to 325°F. Combine all crust ingredients in small bowl. Press crumb mixture evenly onto bottom of ungreased 9-inch springform pan. Bake for 10 minutes. Cool completely.

• Meanwhile, combine sour cream and cream cheese in large bowl. Beat at low speed 1 minute. Add eggs, 1 at a time, beating well after each addition. Add sugar, peanut butter and cornstarch. Continue beating until well mixed. (DO NOT OVERBEAT.) Stir in chocolate chips.

• Spoon filling over cooled crust. Bake for 60 to 80 minutes or until center is almost set. (Cheesecake surface may be slightly cracked and lightly browned.)

• Immediately run knife around inside of pan to loosen sides of cheesecake. Cool 1 hour. Remove sides of pan. Cover; refrigerate until completely cooled (4 hours or overnight). Store covered in refrigerator up to 3 days. Top each serving with whipped cream and cookie crumbs, if desired.

tip:
Substitute graham crackers, gingersnaps or vanilla wafers in the crust. It is easy to crush the crackers or cookies in a food processor or in a heavy resealable plastic food storage bag. Simply crush them with a rolling pin. Just make sure there are no large pieces or the crust may crumble when cut.

tip:
Most cheesecakes will puff up slightly as they bake. When baked sufficiently, the top should no longer be shiny. When you tap the side of the pan, the cheesecake will move but not jiggle. The center will appear softer than the edges and may sink during cooling.

tip:
To freeze, follow directions above for cooling. Wrap cheesecake in plastic food wrap, then in heavy-duty aluminum foil. Label; freeze up to 2 months.

Butter Rum Banana Cake

Preparation time: **45 minutes** | Baking time: **35 minutes** | 18 servings

Cake

1½ cups sugar
 1 cup LAND O LAKES® Butter, softened
 4 eggs
 4 medium (2 cups) ripe bananas, mashed
 ¼ teaspoon rum extract
 3 cups all-purpose flour
1½ teaspoons baking soda
 1 teaspoon baking powder
 1 teaspoon salt
 ½ teaspoon ground cinnamon

Sauce

¾ cup firmly packed brown sugar
 ⅓ cup light corn syrup
 3 tablespoons water
 5 tablespoons LAND O LAKES® Butter
 ¼ cup sweetened condensed milk
 ¼ teaspoon rum extract

Topping

 1 cup LAND O LAKES™ Heavy Whipping Cream
 2 tablespoons powdered sugar

 ½ cup honey-roasted cashews, if desired

• Heat oven to 350°F. Combine sugar and 1 cup butter in large bowl. Beat at medium speed, scraping bowl often, until creamy. Add eggs; continue beating until well mixed. Reduce speed to low; add bananas and rum extract. Beat until well mixed. Add all remaining cake ingredients. Continue beating, scraping bowl often, just until mixed.

• Pour into greased 13×9-inch baking pan. Bake for 35 to 40 minutes or until toothpick inserted in center comes out clean. Cool, uncovered, at least 1 hour.

• Meanwhile, combine brown sugar, corn syrup and water in small saucepan. Cook over medium heat, stirring constantly, until sugar is completely dissolved (3 to 4 minutes). Add 5 tablespoons butter; continue cooking until butter is melted (1 to 2 minutes). Remove from heat; stir in condensed milk and rum extract. Cool 15 minutes.

• Beat whipping cream in chilled small bowl at high speed, scraping bowl often, until soft peaks form. Continue beating, gradually adding powdered sugar, until stiff peaks form.

• To serve, place individual cake servings onto dessert plates. Drizzle with about 1 tablespoon sauce. Dollop with whipped cream; sprinkle with cashews, if desired. Drizzle with additional sauce.

tip:
Store leftovers in refrigerator.

tip:
Leftover ripe bananas can be frozen and used for banana bread, etc. Place unpeeled bananas in resealable plastic freezer bag and freeze. Thaw at room temperature and mash according to recipe.

tip:
To keep bananas from ripening too quickly, place them in the refrigerator until they reach the desired ripeness. The peels may darken but the bananas will ripen more slowly than they would at room temperature.

Chocolate Chai Cupcakes with Cinnamon Buttercream

Preparation time: **1 hour** | Baking time: **19 minutes** | 24 cupcakes

Filling

- ⅓ cup sugar
- 1 (8-ounce) package cream cheese, softened
- 1 egg

Cake

- 1½ cups boiling water
- 5 chai-flavored tea bags
- 1 (18.25-ounce) package chocolate fudge or chocolate cake mix
- ½ cup LAND O LAKES® Butter, melted, cooled slightly
- 3 eggs

Frosting

- 3 tablespoons reserved prepared tea
- ¾ cup milk
- ¼ cup all-purpose flour
- 1½ tablespoons unsweetened cocoa
- 1 cup LAND O LAKES® Butter, softened
- 1 cup sugar
- ¼ teaspoon ground cinnamon

Ground nutmeg or cinnamon, if desired

- Heat oven to 350°F. Line cupcake pan cups with paper liners; set aside.

- Combine all filling ingredients in medium bowl. Beat at medium speed until creamy; set aside.

- Combine boiling water and tea bags in glass measuring cup, let stand 5 minutes. Remove tea bags, squeezing out excess liquid. Add enough water, if necessary, to equal 1½ cups.

- Reserve 3 tablespoons prepared tea; set aside. Place remaining prepared tea in large bowl; add cake mix, melted butter and eggs. Beat at low speed 30 seconds. Beat at medium speed, scraping bowl often, until creamy.

- Spoon about 2 tablespoons cake batter into each paper-lined cup. Top each with 1 tablespoon filling. Spoon additional cake batter over filling until cupcake cups are about two-thirds full. (DO NOT OVERFILL.) (Batter does not have to cover filling completely.) Bake for 19 to 22 minutes or until toothpick inserted in center comes out clean. Cool completely.

- Combine reserved prepared tea and milk in 2-quart saucepan. Add flour and cocoa; whisk until smooth. Cook over medium heat, stirring constantly, until mixture thickens and just comes to a boil (4 to 6 minutes). Remove from heat; cool about 15 minutes.

- Combine 1 cup butter, 1 cup sugar and cinnamon in medium bowl. Beat at high speed until creamy. Continue beating, gradually adding milk mixture, 1 tablespoon at a time, until light and creamy and sugar is dissolved. Frost or pipe cooled cupcakes. Sprinkle with nutmeg, if desired.

tip:
Cupcakes can be made up to 1 week ahead. Freeze in airtight freezer container. Thaw the day of serving.

tip:
To pipe frosting, fit pastry bag with large star tip. Fill pastry bag with frosting and pipe onto cupcakes.

Chocolate Truffle Toffee Cheesecake

Preparation time: **15 minutes** | Baking time: **54 minutes** | **16 servings**

Crust

1⅓ cups (22 cookies) shortbread cookie crumbs

¼ cup LAND O LAKES® Butter, melted

¼ cup sugar

Filling

2 (8-ounce) packages cream cheese, softened

¼ cup sugar

8 (1-ounce) squares semi-sweet baking chocolate, melted

2 eggs

1 teaspoon vanilla

¾ cup milk chocolate English toffee bits

Topping

¾ cup real semi-sweet chocolate chips

½ cup LAND O LAKES™ Heavy Whipping Cream

¼ cup milk chocolate English toffee bits

• Heat oven to 325°F. Combine all crust ingredients in small bowl. Press onto bottom of ungreased 9-inch springform pan with removable bottom. Bake 4 minutes.

• Beat cream cheese and sugar in large bowl until creamy. Add melted chocolate, eggs and vanilla; beat until well mixed. Stir in ¾ cup toffee bits by hand. Spread cream cheese mixture over crust. Continue baking for 50 to 55 minutes or until center is set. Cool in pan 1 hour. Remove from pan.

• Meanwhile, place chocolate chips in small bowl. Place whipping cream in small saucepan; bring to a boil over medium heat (2 to 3 minutes). Pour whipping cream over chocolate chips. Let stand 5 minutes; stir until smooth. Cool until mixture falls in ribbons off spoon (about 1 hour). Spread over cheesecake; sprinkle outer rim of cheesecake with ¼ cup toffee chips. Cover; refrigerate 4 hours or overnight.

tip:

To melt chocolate, place in 1-quart saucepan. Cook, stirring occasionally, over very low heat until melted. Or, place chocolate in microwave-safe bowl. Microwave on MEDIUM (50% power), stirring occasionally, until melted (1 to 2 minutes).

Orange Cream Layer Cake

Preparation time: **45 minutes** | Baking time: **27 minutes** | **12 servings**

Cake

- 1¾ cups all-purpose flour
- 1½ teaspoons baking powder
- ¼ teaspoon baking soda
- ¼ teaspoon salt
- 1½ cups sugar
- ¾ cup LAND O LAKES® Butter, softened
- 1 tablespoon freshly grated orange peel
- 3 eggs
- ¾ cup buttermilk*

Filling

- ⅓ cup powdered sugar
- ¼ cup LAND O LAKES™ Heavy Whipping Cream
- 1 (8-ounce) package cream cheese, softened
- 2 tablespoons frozen orange juice concentrate, thawed
- 1 tablespoon freshly grated orange peel

Frosting

- 1 cup LAND O LAKES™ Heavy Whipping Cream
- 2 tablespoons powdered sugar
- 1 teaspoon freshly grated orange peel

Orange peel, if desired

• Heat oven to 350°F. Grease and flour 2 (9-inch) round cake pans; set aside. Combine flour, baking powder, baking soda and salt in small bowl; set aside.

• Combine 1½ cups sugar, ¾ cup butter and 1 tablespoon orange peel in large bowl. Beat at medium speed, scraping bowl often, until creamy. Add eggs, 1 at a time, beating well after each addition until light and fluffy. Add flour mixture alternately with buttermilk, beating just until combined. Spread batter evenly into prepared pans. Bake for 27 to 32 minutes or until toothpick inserted in center comes out clean. Let stand 10 minutes; remove from pans. Cool completely.

• Meanwhile, combine all filling ingredients in medium bowl. Beat at medium speed until fluffy. Reserve ½ cup filling.

• To assemble cake, place 1 layer onto serving plate. Spread remaining filling over cake. Top with remaining cake layer. Cover; refrigerate while preparing frosting.

• Combine reserved filling and all frosting ingredients in large bowl. Beat at high speed, scraping bowl often, until stiff peaks form. Frost top and sides of cake. Serve immediately or cover and refrigerate for up to 6 hours. Garnish with orange peel, if desired. Store refrigerated.

*Substitute 2 teaspoons vinegar or lemon juice plus enough milk to equal ¾ cup. Let stand 10 minutes.

tip:

For easy holiday entertaining, make the cake layers and filling a day before serving. Tightly wrap cooled cake layers in plastic food wrap. Prepare frosting and assemble cake before serving.

Cinnamony Carrot Cake

Preparation time: **15 minutes** | Baking time: **35 minutes** | **15 servings**

Cake

- 1 (18.25-ounce) package yellow cake mix
- 1¼ cups water
- ½ cup LAND O LAKES® Butter, melted, cooled
- 3 eggs
- 2 cups shredded carrots
- 2 teaspoons ground cinnamon

Frosting

- 4 cups powdered sugar
- ½ cup LAND O LAKES® Butter, softened
- ⅓ cup LAND O LAKES® Sour Cream
- ¾ teaspoon vanilla

• Heat oven to 350°F. Combine all cake ingredients except carrots and cinnamon in large bowl. Beat as directed on cake mix package. Stir in carrots and cinnamon.

• Pour batter into greased 13×9-inch baking pan. Bake for 35 to 40 minutes or until toothpick inserted in center comes out clean. Cool completely.

• Combine all frosting ingredients in large bowl. Beat at medium speed, scraping bowl often, until creamy. Spread cooled cake with frosting.

tip:
One medium carrot will yield about 1 cup shredded carrot.

Toffee-Topped Chocolate Angel Food Cake

Preparation time: **15 minutes** | **16 servings**

Cake

  1 (14.5- to 16-ounce) package angel food cake mix

  ¼ cup unsweetened cocoa

  1 teaspoon almond extract

Frosting

  2 cups LAND O LAKES™ Heavy Whipping Cream

  ¼ cup powdered sugar

  ⅔ cup English toffee bits

  1 teaspoon almond extract

• Combine all cake ingredients in large bowl; prepare according to package directions. Pour batter into 10-inch angel food cake (tube) pan; bake according to package directions. Cool completely.

• Beat whipping cream in chilled small bowl at high speed, scraping bowl often, until soft peaks form. Continue beating, gradually adding powdered sugar, until stiff peaks form. Gently stir in ½ cup toffee bits and 1 teaspoon almond extract.

• Spread top and sides of cake with frosting. Sprinkle top with remaining toffee bits. Store refrigerated.

Caramelized Banana Tart, p. 190

Old-Fashioned Apple Crisp *(opposite page)*, p. 204

PIES AND DESSERTS

Who doesn't love pie and ice cream? And who can turn down a helping of pudding or a crisp? You'll turn every day into a holiday when you serve a homemade dessert.

Pear Hazelnut Crostatas

Preparation time: **25 minutes** | Baking time: **25 minutes** | **4 servings**

¼ cup all-purpose flour
2 tablespoons firmly packed brown sugar
2 tablespoons LAND O LAKES® Butter
2 tablespoons chopped hazelnuts
½ (17.3-ounce) package (1 sheet) frozen puff pastry sheets, thawed
2 ripe but firm medium pears, peeled, sliced crosswise into ¼- to ⅛-inch thick slices
1 tablespoon lemon juice
2 tablespoons sugar

Sugar, if desired
Ice cream, if desired

• Heat oven to 375°F. Combine flour and brown sugar in small bowl. Cut in butter with pastry blender or fork until mixture resembles coarse crumbs. Stir in hazelnuts; set aside.

• Roll out puff pastry sheet on lightly floured surface into a 10-inch square. Cut into 4 equal (5-inch) squares with sharp knife. Place squares onto large ungreased baking sheet. Brush edges lightly with water. Fold in ¾ inch of dough on 2 opposite sides of each square; press firmly. Place baking sheet in refrigerator while preparing pear mixture.

• Combine pears, lemon juice and sugar in large bowl.

• Layer pear slices down center of puff pastry rectangles, keeping pears inside folded edges. Sprinkle each crostata with about 3 tablespoons crumb mixture. Bake for 25 to 27 minutes or until pastry is puffed and golden brown. Cool on wire rack. Sprinkle with sugar, if desired. Serve warm or at room temperature with ice cream, if desired.

tip:
The crostatas can be baked 1 day ahead and stored loosely covered. Reheat in 350°F. oven for 15 minutes just before serving.

tip:
Puff pastry sheets can be found in the freezer section of the grocery store. Once it has thawed, work with 1 pastry sheet at a time and keep the other refrigerated until you're ready to work with it. Gently unfold the pastry sheets to avoid tearing at the folded area; then gently roll out the sheet with a rolling pin on a lightly floured surface to even out the fold's crease.

Pecan Caramel Silk Pie

Preparation time: **35 minutes** | Baking time: **8 minutes** | **12 servings**

Crust

- 1 cup graham cracker crumbs
- ¼ cup finely chopped pecans
- ¼ cup LAND O LAKES® Butter, melted
- 2 tablespoons sugar

Filling

- ¾ cup LAND O LAKES® Butter, softened
- 1 cup sugar
- 2 (1-ounce) squares unsweetened baking chocolate, melted, cooled
- 2 teaspoons vanilla
- ½ cup pasteurized refrigerated real egg product

Topping

- 1 cup LAND O LAKES™ Heavy Whipping Cream
- 1 tablespoon caramel ice cream topping, warmed
- 1 tablespoon chocolate ice cream topping, warmed
- Pecan halves

• Heat oven to 350°F. Stir together all crust ingredients in small bowl. Press into 9-inch pie pan. Bake for 8 to 10 minutes or until lightly browned. Cool completely.

• Meanwhile, combine ¾ cup butter and 1 cup sugar in large bowl. Beat at medium speed, scraping bowl often, until creamy. Stir in melted chocolate and vanilla. Add egg product; continue beating until smooth. Spoon mixture into cooled baked crust. Refrigerate until firm (4 hours or overnight).

• At serving time, beat whipping cream in chilled medium bowl at high speed, scraping bowl often, until stiff peaks form. Dollop or pipe each serving with whipped cream; drizzle with caramel and chocolate toppings. Garnish with pecan halves.

Caramelized Banana Tart

Preparation time: **15 minutes** | Baking time: **30 minutes** | **10 servings**

> 3 tablespoons LAND O LAKES® Butter
> ⅔ cup sugar
> ⅓ cup pecan halves
> 3 large firm bananas
> 2 tablespoons lemon juice
> ½ (17.3-ounce) package (1 sheet) frozen puff pastry sheets, thawed
>
>   Powdered sugar

• Heat oven to 425°F. Melt butter in 11×7-inch baking pan in oven; sprinkle evenly with sugar. Top with pecans.

• Cut bananas diagonally into slices. Place bananas over sugar, overlapping if necessary. Drizzle with lemon juice.

• Unfold thawed pastry; stretch or roll slightly to fit pan. Place pastry over bananas. Tuck edges of pastry in around edges of filling.

• Bake for 30 to 35 minutes or until pastry is golden brown and sauce is bubbly.

• Loosen edges of pan with spatula or knife. Carefully invert onto serving platter. Sprinkle with powdered sugar. Serve warm.

tip:
Make sure thawed puff pastry sheet does not become warm or it may not rise properly. When rolling, work from center of sheet toward edges taking care to keep consistent thickness.

tip:
If using a glass baking dish, reduce oven temperature to 400°F. Bake as directed above.

Blueberry Lemon Parfaits

Preparation time: **15 minutes** | **6 servings**

Butter Nut Crunch

2 tablespoons LAND O LAKES® Butter

¼ cup firmly packed brown sugar

⅓ cup slivered almonds, coarsely chopped*

¼ cup uncooked old-fashioned oats

Lemon Cream

1½ cups LAND O LAKES™ Heavy Whipping Cream

½ cup lemon curd

1 pint fresh blueberries**

• Line a 15×10×1-inch jelly-roll pan with aluminum foil; set aside.

• Melt butter in 10-inch skillet until sizzling; add brown sugar. Cook, stirring constantly, over medium-high heat until bubbling (1 minute). Add almonds and oats; stir. Pour onto prepared pan; cool completely. Break into chunks; store in container with tight-fitting lid until ready to assemble parfaits.

• Beat whipping cream in chilled medium bowl, scraping bowl often, until soft peaks form. Add lemon curd; continue beating until stiff peaks form.

• To assemble each parfait, layer ½ cup lemon cream, ⅓ cup berries and 2 heaping tablespoons butter nut crunch in each of 6 (8- to 10-ounce) plastic cups or dessert glasses.

*Substitute pecans or walnuts.

**Substitute fresh raspberries or small blackberries.

tip:

Prepare up to 1 hour ahead. Cover each glass with plastic food wrap; refrigerate.

Chocolate Bread Pudding

Preparation time: **15 minutes** | Baking time: **1 hour 10 minutes** | **8 servings**

Pudding

- 3 cups milk
- 4 (1-ounce) squares semi-sweet baking chocolate
- 8 slices (4 cups) day-old white bread, cut into ½-inch cubes
- ¼ cup sugar
- 2 eggs
- 3 tablespoons LAND O LAKES® Butter, melted
- 1 teaspoon ground cinnamon

Sauce

- 1 cup chocolate fudge ice cream topping or chocolate-flavored syrup, warmed
- 1 tablespoon bourbon, if desired*

Topping

- ½ cup LAND O LAKES™ Heavy Whipping Cream, whipped, sweetened
- Ground cinnamon, if desired

• Heat oven to 350°F. Combine milk and chocolate in 2-quart saucepan. Cook over medium heat, stirring occasionally, until chocolate is melted (5 to 7 minutes). (DO NOT BOIL.) Remove from heat. Stir milk mixture with wire whisk until well blended. Stir in bread cubes; set aside.

• Stir together sugar, eggs, butter and cinnamon in large bowl; stir in bread mixture. Place mixture into greased 1½-quart casserole. Place casserole in 13×9-inch baking pan. Place on oven rack; pour boiling water into baking pan to within 1 inch of top of casserole.

• Bake for 70 to 80 minutes or until knife inserted in center comes out clean. If browning too quickly, cover with aluminum foil. Let stand 10 minutes.

• Stir together chocolate fudge topping and bourbon, if desired, in small bowl. Serve warm bread pudding with sauce and sweetened whipped cream. Sprinkle with cinnamon, if desired.

*Substitute 1 teaspoon brandy extract.

Decadent Chocolate Custard

Preparation time: **10 minutes** | Cooking time: **10 minutes** | **6 (3-ounce) servings**

> 1 cup LAND O LAKES™ Heavy Whipping Cream
> ⅓ cup milk
> 6 ounces good quality semi-sweet chocolate, chopped
> 4 egg yolks

• Place cream and milk in heavy 2-quart saucepan. Cook over medium-high heat, stirring occasionally, until mixture just comes to a boil (2 to 3 minutes). Immediately remove from heat. Add chocolate; whisk until melted and smooth.

• Whisk yolks in large bowl just to blend. Gradually whisk warm chocolate mixture into beaten yolks. Return chocolate mixture to same saucepan. Cook over medium heat, stirring constantly, until mixture thickens and just begins to bubble (8 to 10 minutes). (DO NOT BOIL.)

• Pour custard evenly into 6 (3-ounce) custard cups. Cool completely. Cover; chill 1 hour or until serving time.

Grilled Caramel Peaches

Preparation time: **20 minutes** | Grilling time: **8 minutes** | **4 servings**

  2 large (about 2 cups) peaches, cut into ½-inch slices*
¼ cup firmly packed brown sugar
  2 tablespoons LAND O LAKES® Butter, softened
¼ teaspoon ground cinnamon
¼ cup LAND O LAKES™ Fat Free Half & Half or Half & Half

• Heat gas grill on medium or charcoal grill until coals are ash white. Divide all ingredients except half & half equally onto 2 (12-inch) lengths of heavy-duty aluminum foil. Cover each with another 12-inch length of foil. Seal edges by folding over twice.

• Place aluminum foil packets onto grill. Grill, turning halfway through grilling, until peaches are tender (8 to 10 minutes).

• Carefully slit open top of aluminum foil packet; spoon peach mixture from packets into serving dishes. Pour 1 tablespoon half & half over each serving.

*Substitute 2 cups frozen sliced peaches, thawed.

tip:
Spoon warm peaches over vanilla ice cream for a tasty treat.

Mixed-Berry Almond Pie

Preparation time: **45 minutes** | Baking time: **40 minutes** | **8 servings**

Crust

   2 cups all-purpose flour
   ¼ cup finely chopped almonds
   ¼ teaspoon salt
   ⅔ cup cold LAND O LAKES® Butter
   5 to 7 tablespoons cold water

Filling

   6 cups mixed fresh or frozen berries
      (blueberries, blackberries, raspberries,
      sliced strawberries)
   ½ cup sugar
   ¼ cup cornstarch
   ¼ teaspoon almond extract

   1 egg, slightly beaten

• Heat oven to 425°F. Combine flour, almonds and salt in large bowl; cut in butter with pastry blender or fork until mixture resembles coarse crumbs. Stir in enough water just until flour is moistened. Divide dough in half. Shape each half into ball; flatten slightly. Wrap 1 ball of dough in plastic food wrap; refrigerate.

• Roll out 1 ball of dough on lightly floured surface into 12-inch circle. Fold into quarters. Place dough into ungreased 9-inch pie pan; unfold, pressing firmly against bottom and sides. Trim crust to ½ inch from edge of pan; set aside.

• Combine all filling ingredients except egg in large bowl; toss lightly to coat berries. Spoon into prepared crust.

• Roll out remaining ball of dough on lightly floured surface into 12-inch circle. Cut out 12 (1-inch) strips with sharp knife or pastry wheel. Place 6 strips 1 inch apart over filling. Place remaining 6 strips at an angle to strips already in place. Trim ends. Fold remaining edge of bottom crust over strips; build up an edge. Crimp or flute edge. Brush crust with beaten egg.

• Bake for 40 to 50 minutes or until crust is lightly browned and juice begins to bubble. (If browning too quickly, cover with aluminum foil.)

tip:
If using frozen fruit, increase baking time by 15 minutes.

Italian Vanilla Cream

Preparation time: **10 minutes** | **6 servings**

  ¼ cup milk
  1 (¼-ounce) envelope unflavored gelatin
  2 cups (1 pint) LAND O LAKES™ Heavy Whipping Cream
  ½ cup sugar
  2 teaspoons vanilla

     Fresh raspberries, strawberries and/or blueberries

• Pour milk into medium bowl; sprinkle with gelatin. Let stand until gelatin is softened (2 minutes).

• Place whipping cream and sugar in 1-quart saucepan. Cook over low heat, stirring constantly, until sugar is dissolved (4 minutes). Remove from heat.

• Add cream mixture to gelatin mixture; mix well. Stir in vanilla.

• Pour mixture evenly into 6 (6-ounce) ungreased ramekins or custard cups. Cover; refrigerate until firm (4 hours or overnight).

• Run knife around edges of each ramekin. Unmold onto individual serving plates; surround with fresh berries.

Chocolate Raspberry Mousse

Preparation time: **20 minutes** | **4 servings**

½ cup LAND O LAKES® Butter, softened

⅓ cup sugar

2 (1-ounce) squares semi-sweet baking chocolate, melted, cooled

½ cup pasteurized refrigerated real egg product

2 teaspoons raspberry liqueur, if desired

½ pint raspberries

• Combine butter and sugar in small bowl. Beat at medium speed, scraping bowl often, until creamy. Add chocolate; continue beating, scraping bowl often, until well mixed. Add eggs; continue beating, scraping bowl often, until very creamy. Stir in raspberry liqueur, if desired.

• To serve, place 4 raspberries in bottom of each of 4 parfait glasses. Top with ¼ cup chocolate mousse, 4 raspberries and ¼ cup chocolate mousse. Garnish with remaining raspberries. Store refrigerated. Any remaining mousse can be stored in the refrigerator up to 2 days.

Pumpkin Ginger Tart

Preparation time: **25 minutes** | Baking time: **55 minutes** | **8 servings**

Crust

- 1 cup all-purpose flour
- ⅛ teaspoon salt
- ⅓ cup cold LAND O LAKES® Butter, cut into pieces
- 1 teaspoon freshly grated gingerroot*
- 3 to 4 tablespoons cold water

Filling

- 1 (15-ounce) can pumpkin
- ½ cup sugar
- 2 teaspoons freshly grated gingerroot**
- 1 teaspoon vanilla
- ½ teaspoon ground cinnamon
- 2 eggs, slightly beaten
- ½ cup LAND O LAKES™ Heavy Whipping Cream

Streusel

- ¾ cup all-purpose flour
- ⅓ cup firmly packed brown sugar
- ¼ cup cold LAND O LAKES® Butter, cut into pieces

Topping

- 1 cup LAND O LAKES™ Heavy Whipping Cream
- 1 tablespoon powdered sugar

Grated orange peel, if desired

• Heat oven to 375°F. Stir together 1 cup flour and salt in large bowl; cut in ⅓ cup butter with pastry blender or fork until mixture resembles coarse crumbs. Mix in 1 teaspoon gingerroot and enough water with fork until flour is just moistened. Pat into ungreased 10-inch tart pan with removable bottom or 9-inch glass pie pan. Bake for 10 to 15 minutes or until crust just begins to brown.

• Combine pumpkin, sugar, 2 teaspoons gingerroot, vanilla and cinnamon in large bowl. Stir in eggs just until well mixed. Stir in ½ cup whipping cream. Pour pumpkin mixture into baked crust. Cover edge of crust with aluminum foil. Bake for 30 to 35 minutes or until set around edge.

• Meanwhile, combine ¾ cup flour and brown sugar in small bowl. Cut in ¼ cup butter with pastry blender or fork until mixture resembles fine crumbs. Sprinkle streusel over hot, partially baked filling. Continue baking for 15 to 20 minutes or until knife inserted in center comes out clean. Cool 30 minutes.

• Before serving, beat all topping ingredients in chilled small bowl at high speed, scraping bowl often, until stiff peaks form. To serve, dollop each serving with topping mixture. Garnish with orange peel, if desired.

*Substitute ¼ teaspoon ground ginger.

**Substitute ½ teaspoon ground ginger.

tip:
Peppery and slightly sweet, gingerroot has a tan skin and yellow to ivory flesh. Look for the gnarled root in the produce section of your grocery store. Be sure to peel gingerroot before grating.

Old-Fashioned Apple Crisp

Preparation time: **20 minutes** | Baking time: **25 minutes** | **6 servings**

 6 medium (6 cups) apples, peeled, cored, sliced
 ¾ cup firmly packed brown sugar
 ¾ cup uncooked old-fashioned oats
 ½ cup all-purpose flour
 1 teaspoon ground cinnamon
 ½ cup cold LAND O LAKES® Butter

 Vanilla ice cream, if desired

• Heat oven to 375°F. Place apples into ungreased 9-inch square (2-quart) baking dish.

• Combine brown sugar, oats, flour and cinnamon in medium bowl; cut in butter with pastry blender or fork until mixture resembles coarse crumbs. Sprinkle sugar mixture over apples. Bake for 25 to 35 minutes or until apples are tender and topping is golden brown.

• Serve warm with ice cream, if desired.

tip:
Select an apple variety recommended for baking, or use a combination of baking apples such as Granny Smith, McIntosh and Braeburn.

Streusel Blueberry Buckle

Preparation time: **20 minutes** | Baking time: **40 minutes** | 9 servings

Cake

   2 cups all-purpose flour
   ¾ cup sugar
   ½ cup milk
   ¼ cup LAND O LAKES® Butter, softened
   1 egg
   2 teaspoons baking powder
   ½ teaspoon salt
   ¼ teaspoon ground nutmeg
   1 cup fresh or frozen blueberries

Topping

   ½ cup sugar
   ⅓ cup all-purpose flour
   ½ teaspoon ground cinnamon
   ½ teaspoon ground nutmeg
   ¼ cup LAND O LAKES® Butter, softened

• Heat oven to 375°F. Grease and flour 8-inch square baking pan; set aside.

• Combine all cake ingredients except blueberries in large bowl. Beat at low speed, scraping bowl often, until well mixed. Gently stir in blueberries by hand. Spread batter into prepared baking pan.

• Stir together all streusel ingredients except butter in small bowl; cut in butter with pastry blender or fork until mixture resembles coarse crumbs. Sprinkle over batter. Bake for 40 to 45 minutes or until toothpick inserted in center comes out clean.

Hazelnut Orange Coconut Bars, p. 212

Double Chocolate Peanut Butter Bars *(opposite page)*, p. 222

BROWNIES AND BARS

These one-pan desserts are delicious enough to serve your guests, casual enough for anytime snacking, and easy enough to make for any occasion, from pot lucks to bake sales.

Cranberry Pistachio Bars

Preparation time: **15 minutes** | Baking time: **20 minutes** | **16 bars**

Crust
- 1 cup all-purpose flour
- ⅓ cup firmly packed brown sugar
- ½ cup LAND O LAKES® Butter

Topping
- 1 egg, beaten
- ¼ cup sugar
- ¼ cup firmly packed brown sugar
- 2 tablespoons all-purpose flour
- ½ teaspoon vanilla
- 1 cup chopped fresh cranberries
- ¼ cup coarsely chopped pistachio nuts

Powdered sugar

• Heat oven to 375°F. Combine 1 cup flour and ⅓ cup brown sugar in small bowl. Cut in butter with pastry blender or fork until mixture resembles coarse crumbs. Press onto bottom of ungreased 8-inch square baking pan. Bake for 12 to 15 minutes or until lightly browned.

• Meanwhile, combine egg, sugar, ¼ cup brown sugar, 2 tablespoons flour and vanilla in same small bowl. Stir in cranberries and nuts. Pour over hot, partially baked crust. Continue baking for 20 to 25 minutes or until center appears set. Cool completely on wire rack. Sprinkle with powdered sugar; cut into bars with sharp knife.

tip:
For the best flavor and texture, store sealed packages of nuts in a cool, dark place. Once you've opened the package, place the nuts in a container with a tight-fitting lid and keep them in the refrigerator for up to 6 months or in the freezer for up to 1 year.

Fudgy Raspberry Brownies

Preparation time: **15 minutes** | Baking time: **40 minutes** | **36 brownies**

Brownie

- 1 cup LAND O LAKES® Butter
- 4 (1-ounce) squares unsweetened baking chocolate
- 2 cups sugar
- 4 eggs
- 1 teaspoon vanilla
- 1 teaspoon almond extract
- 1½ cups all-purpose flour
- ¼ teaspoon salt
- ½ cup seedless raspberry jam

Glaze

- ¼ cup LAND O LAKES™ Heavy Whipping Cream
- 4 (1-ounce) squares semi-sweet baking chocolate

• Heat oven to 350°F. Place butter and unsweetened chocolate in medium microwave-safe bowl. Microwave on HIGH (100% power) for 1 minute; stir. Microwave 30 seconds; stir until smooth; set aside.

• Combine sugar, eggs, vanilla and almond extract in large bowl. Beat at medium speed until well mixed. Add melted chocolate mixture; continue beating until well mixed. Reduce speed to low; add flour and salt. Beat just until mixed. Spread batter into greased 13×9-inch baking pan.

• Stir jam until smooth. Drop tablespoonfuls of jam evenly over batter. Swirl jam through batter using knife. Bake for 40 to 45 minutes or until set and brownies begin to pull away from sides of pan. (DO NOT OVERBAKE.) Cool completely.

• Place whipping cream in 1-quart saucepan. Cook over medium heat just until cream begins to boil (1 to 2 minutes). Add semi-sweet chocolate; remove from heat. Stir with wire whisk until smooth. Spread over brownies.

tip:

For easy pan removal and cutting, line baking pan with aluminum foil, leaving 1-inch overhang on ends; lightly grease foil. Once brownies are cooled and frosted, remove brownies by lifting foil at edges. Cut into bars.

Hazelnut Orange Coconut Bars

Preparation time: **25 minutes** | Baking time: **40 minutes** | **36 bars**

Crust

2 cups all-purpose flour

½ cup sugar

1 tablespoon freshly grated orange peel

1 cup LAND O LAKES® Butter

Filling

2 eggs, slightly beaten

¾ cup sugar

¼ cup orange juice

2 tablespoons all-purpose flour

1 tablespoon freshly grated orange peel

½ teaspoon baking powder

½ cup sweetened flaked coconut

⅓ cup finely chopped hazelnuts

Powdered sugar

• Heat oven to 350°F. Combine 2 cups flour, ½ cup sugar and 1 tablespoon orange peel in large bowl. Cut in butter with pastry blender or fork until mixture resembles coarse crumbs. Press onto bottom of ungreased 13×9-inch baking pan. Bake for 20 to 22 minutes or until light golden brown.

• Meanwhile, combine all filling ingredients except coconut, hazelnuts and powdered sugar in large bowl; mix well. Stir in coconut.

• Pour over hot, partially baked crust. Sprinkle with hazelnuts. Bake for 20 to 25 minutes or until center is set. Cool completely. Sprinkle with powdered sugar.

tip:

Hazelnuts, also called filberts, are sold with the brown outer skin removed or with it still on the nut. Since the skin has a bitter flavor, look for nuts that already have the skin removed. If you purchase hazelnuts that still have a skin, heat them in a 350°F. oven for 10 to 15 minutes or until the skins begin to flake. Place the warm nuts, a handful at a time, in a clean dish towel and rub to remove most of the skin.

Classic Chocolate Brownies

Preparation time: **20 minutes** | Baking time: **25 minutes** | **25 brownies**

    ½ cup LAND O LAKES® Butter
    2 (1-ounce) squares unsweetened baking chocolate
    1 (1-ounce) square semi-sweet baking chocolate
 1¼ cups sugar
 1½ teaspoons vanilla
    3 eggs
 1¼ cups all-purpose flour
    ¼ teaspoon salt

    Powdered sugar, if desired

• Heat oven to 350°F. Grease bottom only of 8- or 9-inch square baking pan; set aside.

• Melt butter, unsweetened chocolate and semi-sweet chocolate in 2-quart saucepan over low heat, stirring occasionally, until smooth (4 to 7 minutes). Remove from heat.

• Stir in sugar and vanilla. Add eggs, 1 at a time, mixing well after each addition. Stir in flour and salt; mix just until all ingredients are moistened and brownie mixture is smooth. (DO NOT OVERMIX.)

• Spread brownie mixture into prepared pan. Bake for 25 to 32 minutes or until brownies just begin to pull away from sides of pan. (DO NOT OVERBAKE.) Cool completely. Sprinkle with powdered sugar, if desired.

Caramel 'n Chocolate Pecan Bars

Preparation time: **15 minutes** | Baking time: **18 minutes** | 36 bars

Crust
 2 cups all-purpose flour
 1 cup firmly packed brown sugar
 ½ cup LAND O LAKES® Butter, softened
 1 cup pecan halves

Caramel Layer
 ⅔ cup LAND O LAKES® Butter
 ½ cup firmly packed brown sugar

Chocolate
 1 cup milk chocolate chips

• Heat oven to 350°F. Combine all crust ingredients except pecans in large bowl. Beat at medium speed until mixture resembles fine crumbs.

• Press onto bottom of ungreased 13×9-inch baking pan. Place pecans evenly over unbaked crust.

• Combine ⅔ cup butter and ½ cup brown sugar in 1-quart saucepan. Cook over medium heat, stirring constantly, until entire surface of mixture begins to boil. Boil 1 minute, stirring constantly. Pour mixture evenly over pecans and crust.

• Bake for 18 to 22 minutes or until entire caramel layer is bubbly. (DO NOT OVERBAKE.) Remove from oven. Immediately sprinkle with chips; allow to melt slightly. Swirl melted chips over bars leaving some whole for marbled effect. Cool completely; cut into bars.

tip:
Store at room temperature in loosely covered container.

Mango Bars

Preparation time: **25 minutes** | Baking time: **37 minutes** | **36 bars**

Crust

2 cups all-purpose flour

¾ cup sugar

¼ teaspoon salt

¾ cup LAND O LAKES® Butter

Filling

2 medium (2 cups) fresh mangoes, cut into ½-inch cubes*

1 cup peach preserves, warmed

½ cup slivered almonds, toasted, finely chopped

Glaze

1 cup powdered sugar

2 teaspoons freshly grated lemon peel

½ teaspoon vanilla

1 to 2 tablespoons LAND O LAKES™ Fat Free Half & Half or milk

• Heat oven to 375°F. Combine flour, sugar and salt in large bowl. Cut in butter with pastry blender or fork until mixture resembles coarse crumbs. Reserve ½ cup crumb mixture; set aside. Press remaining crumb mixture onto bottom of ungreased 13×9-inch baking pan. Bake for 16 to 18 minutes or until edges are lightly browned. Remove from oven.

• Top hot, partially baked crust with mangoes and preserves. Combine reserved crumb mixture and almonds; sprinkle over preserves. Bake for 21 to 23 minutes or until crumbs are golden. Cool completely.

• Combine powdered sugar, lemon peel and vanilla in small bowl. Stir in enough half & half for desired drizzling consistency. Drizzle over cooled bars.

*Substitute 1 (24-ounce) jar refrigerated mango in light syrup, drained.

tip:
To toast almonds, heat oven to 350°F. Spread almonds onto ungreased 15×10×1-inch jelly-roll pan. Bake for 5 to 8 minutes, stirring occasionally, or until golden brown.

tip:
Fully ripe mangoes should be green/yellow to red in color, smell fruity and feel fairly firm when gently pressed. Avoid any that are very soft or bruised. If the mangoes at your grocery store are not yet ripe, place them in a paper bag and let them ripen at room temperature for a day or two.

Brown Sugar Praline Bars

Preparation time: **20 minutes** | Baking time: **15 minutes** | 48 bars

Bar

½ cup LAND O LAKES® Butter
½ cup firmly packed brown sugar
1 teaspoon vanilla
1 egg
1 cup all-purpose flour
¼ teaspoon baking powder
⅛ teaspoon salt
¼ cup chopped pecans
¼ cup English toffee bits

Topping

1 (10-ounce) package real semi-sweet chocolate and white baking chips*
2 tablespoons finely chopped pecans
2 tablespoons English toffee bits

• Heat oven to 350°F. Melt butter in 2-quart saucepan. Remove from heat; stir in brown sugar and vanilla. Add egg; mix well. Add flour, baking powder and salt; stir until well mixed. Stir in ¼ cup pecans and ¼ cup toffee bits.

• Spread batter into greased 13×9-inch baking pan. Bake for 15 to 18 minutes or until edges are lightly browned and begin to pull away from sides of pan. Immediately sprinkle with chips; let stand 3 minutes. Swirl chips slightly with knife for marbled effect. Sprinkle remaining topping ingredients over melted chocolate.

• Let stand until chocolate is set (1 to 2 hours). Cut into 24 squares. Cut each square into 2 triangles.

*Substitute ¾ cup real semi-sweet chocolate chips and ¾ cup white baking chips.

Tangy Lemon Bars

Preparation time: **30 minutes** | Baking time: **41 minutes** | 36 bars

Crust

2 cups all-purpose flour
¾ cup sugar
¾ cup LAND O LAKES® Butter, softened

Filling

2 cups sugar
¼ cup lemon juice
4 eggs
2 teaspoons freshly grated lemon peel
⅛ teaspoon salt
¼ cup all-purpose flour
1 teaspoon baking powder

Glaze

1 cup powdered sugar
1 tablespoon LAND O LAKES® Butter, softened
½ teaspoon vanilla
1½ to 2 tablespoons lemon juice

• Heat oven to 350°F. Combine all crust ingredients in large bowl. Beat at medium speed, scraping bowl often, until mixture resembles fine crumbs.

• Press mixture onto bottom of ungreased 13×9-inch baking pan. Bake for 18 to 22 minutes or until edges are very lightly browned.

• Meanwhile, combine all filling ingredients except flour and baking powder in same bowl. Beat at medium speed until well mixed. Reduce speed to low; add ¼ cup flour and baking powder. Beat until well mixed. Pour filling over hot, partially baked crust. Continue baking for 23 to 25 minutes or until top is golden brown. Cool completely.

• Combine all glaze ingredients except lemon juice in small bowl. Beat at low speed, gradually adding enough lemon juice and scraping bowl often, until desired glazing consistency. Drizzle over cooled bars. Cut into bars.

tip:

To cut bars into diamonds, make diagonal cuts across the length of the pan. Make a second set of cuts parallel to the short side of the pan.

Double Chocolate Peanut Butter Bars

Preparation time: **10 minutes** | Baking time: **20 minutes** | **35 bars**

- ½ cup LAND O LAKES® Butter, softened
- ½ cup chunky peanut butter
- 1 cup firmly packed brown sugar
- 2 eggs
- 1 teaspoon vanilla
- 1¾ cups all-purpose flour
- ½ teaspoon baking powder
- ¼ teaspoon baking soda
- 1 cup mini real semi-sweet chocolate chips
- 2 tablespoons sugar
- 35 milk chocolate candy kisses

• Heat oven to 350°F. Line 13×9-inch baking pan with aluminum foil, leaving a 1-inch overhang; set aside.

• Combine butter, peanut butter and brown sugar in large bowl. Beat at medium speed, scraping bowl often, until creamy. Add eggs and vanilla; continue beating until well mixed. Reduce speed to low; add flour, baking powder and baking soda. Beat until well mixed. Stir in chocolate chips.

• Pat dough into prepared pan. Sprinkle with sugar. Bake for 20 to 22 minutes or until golden brown. Cool in pan 5 minutes. Immediately press evenly spaced chocolate candies into warm bars. Cool completely. Remove bars from pan; cut into bars, cutting between candies.

tip:
Peanut butter was first developed in 1890 and promoted at the St. Louis World's Fair in 1904. It's made from ground peanuts, vegetable oil and salt. Sometimes sugar and additives are added to make it creamier or to prevent the oil from separating. Natural peanut butter should be refrigerated after opening. Most other peanut butters keep up to 6 months at room temperature.

Chewy Saucepan Blondies

Preparation time: **15 minutes** | Baking time: **22 minutes** | **36 bars**

½ cup LAND O LAKES® Butter
2 cups firmly packed brown sugar
2 eggs
1 tablespoon vanilla
2 cups all-purpose flour
½ teaspoon salt
½ cup chopped pecans

Powdered sugar

• Heat oven to 350°F. Melt butter in 2-quart saucepan over medium heat (2 to 3 minutes). Add brown sugar; mix well. Cool 10 minutes. Stir in eggs and vanilla. Add flour and salt; mix well. Stir in pecans.

• Spread batter into lightly greased 13×9-inch baking pan. Bake for 22 to 27 minutes or until set. Cool completely. Sprinkle with powdered sugar.

Simple Fudgy Saucepan Brownies

Preparation time: **15 minutes** | Baking time: **23 minutes** | **16 brownies**

Brownie

½ cup LAND O LAKES® Butter
2 (1-ounce) squares unsweetened baking chocolate
1 cup sugar
¾ cup all-purpose flour
2 eggs

Frosting

¼ cup LAND O LAKES® Butter
3 tablespoons milk
1 (1-ounce) square unsweetened baking chocolate
2½ cups powdered sugar
½ teaspoon vanilla

• Heat oven to 350°F. Combine ½ cup butter and 2 squares chocolate in 2-quart saucepan. Cook over medium heat, stirring constantly, until melted (3 to 5 minutes). Stir in all remaining brownie ingredients until well mixed.

• Spread into greased 8-inch square baking pan. Bake for 23 to 27 minutes or until brownies begin to pull away from sides of pan.

• Meanwhile, combine ¼ cup butter, milk and 1 square chocolate in same saucepan. Cook over medium heat, stirring occasionally, until mixture comes to a full boil (2 to 3 minutes). Remove from heat. Add powdered sugar; beat until smooth. Stir in vanilla. Spread over warm brownies. Cool; cut into squares.

Apricot Oatmeal Bars

Preparation time: **30 minutes** | Baking time: **22 minutes** | **36 bars**

Crumb Mixture

1¼ cups all-purpose flour
1¼ cups uncooked quick-cooking oats
¾ cup LAND O LAKES® Butter, melted
½ cup sugar
2 teaspoons vanilla
½ teaspoon baking soda
¼ teaspoon salt

Filling

1 (10-ounce) jar (¾ cup) apricot preserves
½ cup sweetened flaked coconut

• Heat oven to 350°F. Combine all crumb mixture ingredients in large bowl. Beat at low speed until mixture resembles coarse crumbs.

• Reserve 1 cup crumb mixture. Press remaining crumb mixture onto bottom of greased 13×9-inch baking pan.

• Spread apricot preserves to within ½ inch from edge of crust; sprinkle with reserved crumb mixture and coconut. Bake for 22 to 27 minutes or until edges are lightly browned. Cool completely; cut into bars.

Golden Almond Bars

Preparation time: **15 minutes** | Baking time: **20 minutes** | 48 bars

- 1 cup LAND O LAKES® Butter, softened
- 1 cup sugar
- 1 egg, separated
- 1 teaspoon almond extract
- 2 cups all-purpose flour
- 1 tablespoon water
- ½ cup sliced almonds

• Heat oven to 350°F. Combine butter, sugar, egg yolk and almond extract in large bowl. Beat at medium speed, scraping bowl often, until well mixed. Reduce speed to low; add flour. Beat until well mixed.

• Press dough onto bottom of greased 15×10×1 inch jelly-roll pan. Beat together egg white and water with fork in small bowl. Brush over dough; sprinkle with almonds. Bake for 20 to 25 minutes or until lightly browned. Cool completely; cut into bars.

Lemon Clove Cookie Sandwiches, p. 240

Peanut Butter Cookie Cups *(opposite page)*, p. 244

COOKIES
AND CANDIES

Your cookie jar will become the focal point of the kitchen when you keep it full of yummy things to munch on, especially for quick pick-me-ups. Slip a few of these goodies into lunchboxes, too!

Chocolate Dipped Cut-Outs

Preparation time: **35 minutes** | Baking time: **7 minutes per pan** | **6 dozen cookies**

Cookie

  1 cup LAND O LAKES® Butter, softened
  1 cup sugar
  1 egg
  2 tablespoons milk
  1 teaspoon vanilla
  2 cups all-purpose flour
  ½ cup unsweetened cocoa
  1 teaspoon baking powder
  ¼ teaspoon salt

Coating

  Nonpareils or decorator coarse-grain
    sugar, if desired
  2 cups real semi-sweet chocolate chips
  2 tablespoons shortening

• Combine butter and sugar in large bowl; beat at medium speed until creamy. Add egg, milk and vanilla; continue beating until well mixed. Reduce speed to low; add all remaining cookie ingredients. Beat until well mixed.

• Divide dough in half. Wrap each half in plastic food wrap; refrigerate until firm (at least 1 hour).

• Heat oven to 350°F. Roll out dough on lightly floured surface, one-half at a time (keeping remaining dough refrigerated), to ¼-inch thickness. Cut with 2-inch cookie cutter. Place 1 inch apart onto ungreased cookie sheets. Bake for 7 to 8 minutes or until edges are firm. Let stand 1 minute. Remove from cookie sheets. Cool completely.

• Place nonpareils in small shallow dish; set aside. Combine chocolate chips and shortening in 1-quart saucepan. Cook, stirring occasionally, over low heat until chocolate melts. Remove from heat. Dip half of each cookie into chocolate mixture. Immediately roll chocolate-coated edges of cookie in nonpareils, if desired. Let stand on waxed paper until set.

tip:
Your favorite shaped 2-inch cookie cutter can be used.

tip:
Cut-out cookies seem to brighten any celebration. For best results, roll dough on a lightly floured surface from the center to the edges. Measure thickness as you go to assure perfect results. Cut dough into shapes using floured cookie cutters, cutting as close together as possible. Use a pancake turner or wide metal spatula to transfer them from the floured surface to the cookie sheet.

Maple Moons

Preparation time: **1 hour** | Baking time: **8 minutes per pan** | **6 dozen cookies**

Cookie

- ¾ cup LAND O LAKES® Butter, softened
- 1 (3-ounce) package cream cheese, softened
- 1 cup firmly packed brown sugar
- 1 teaspoon maple flavoring
- 2¼ cups all-purpose flour
- ½ teaspoon baking soda

Drizzle

- 1½ cups powdered sugar
- 1½ teaspoons maple flavoring
- 3 to 5 teaspoons water

- ⅔ cup real semi-sweet chocolate chips, melted

• Combine butter and cream cheese in large bowl; beat at medium speed until creamy. Add brown sugar and 1 teaspoon maple flavoring; continue beating until smooth. Reduce speed to low; add flour and baking soda. Continue beating until well mixed. Cover; refrigerate until firm (30 minutes).

• Heat oven to 350°F. Shape dough into 1-inch balls. Roll each ball into a 3-inch rope. Place onto ungreased cookie sheets. Form into crescent shape; pinch ends and flatten middle slightly. Bake for 8 to 10 minutes or until edges are lightly browned. Cool 1 minute; remove from cookie sheets. Place onto wire racks over waxed paper; cool completely.

• Combine powdered sugar, 1½ teaspoons maple flavoring and enough water for desired drizzling consistency in small bowl with wire whisk until smooth. Drizzle over cooled cookies; drizzle with melted chocolate. Let stand until chocolate is set (2 hours). Store cookies between sheets of waxed paper in container with tight-fitting lid.

tip:

To melt chocolate for drizzle, place chocolate chips in small resealable plastic food storage bag. Microwave on MEDIUM (50% power) until chips are melted (1½ to 2 minutes). Snip small hole in 1 corner of bag. Drizzle chocolate over cookies.

Cappuccino Caramels

Preparation time: **25 minutes** | Cooking time: **51 minutes** | **64 candies**

  ½ cup chopped pecans or walnuts
  3 cups firmly packed brown sugar
  1 tablespoon ground cinnamon
  1 tablespoon ground espresso powder or instant coffee granules
  1 cup LAND O LAKES® Butter
  2 cups LAND O LAKES™ Half & Half
  1 cup light corn syrup
  1 teaspoon vanilla

• Line 8-inch square pan with aluminum foil, extending foil over edges of pan. Butter foil. Sprinkle pecans over bottom of pan; set aside.

• Combine brown sugar, cinnamon and espresso powder in small bowl. Melt butter in 4-quart saucepan over low heat; add brown sugar mixture, half & half and corn syrup. Increase heat to medium-high. Cook, stirring constantly, until mixture comes to a boil (6 to 8 minutes).

• Reduce heat to medium. Continue cooking, stirring occasionally, until candy thermometer registers 242°F. or small amount of mixture dropped into ice water forms a firm ball (40 to 45 minutes). Remove from heat; stir in vanilla. Carefully pour over pecans in prepared pan. Cool completely.

• Remove caramels from pan using foil. Cut into 1-inch square pieces with buttered knife. Individually wrap pieces in waxed paper or plastic food wrap. Store refrigerated.

tip:
To make cleaning of candy-making utensils easy, place them in the used saucepan and fill with hot water. Bring the water to a boil. Reduce heat to medium-low. Cook until hardened candy is dissolved. Wash the saucepan and utensils in hot soapy water.

Pistachio Cream Sandwich Cookies

Preparation time: **50 minutes** | Baking time: **8 minutes per pan** | **48 sandwich cookies**

Cookie

- ¾ cup LAND O LAKES® Butter, softened
- ¾ cup powdered sugar
- 1 egg
- 1½ cups all-purpose flour
- ¼ teaspoon salt
- ½ cup finely chopped pistachio nuts

Filling

- 1¼ cups powdered sugar
- ¼ cup LAND O LAKES® Butter, softened
- ½ teaspoon vanilla
- 2 to 4 teaspoons LAND O LAKES™ Fat Free Half & Half or milk
- 2 tablespoons finely chopped pistachio nuts

• Combine ¾ cup butter and ¾ cup powdered sugar in large bowl. Beat on medium speed, scraping bowl often, until well mixed. Add egg; continue beating until combined. Reduce speed to low; add flour and salt. Beat until well mixed. Wrap in plastic food wrap. Refrigerate until firm (at least 1 hour).

• Heat oven to 350°F. Place ½ cup chopped pistachio nuts in small bowl. Shape dough into ½-inch balls. Roll each in pistachio nuts. Place 1 inch apart onto ungreased cookie sheets. Flatten each cookie with bottom of glass dipped in sugar.

• Bake for 7 to 8 minutes or until edges are lightly browned. Transfer to wire rack. Cool completely.

• Combine 1¼ cups powdered sugar, ¼ cup butter, vanilla and enough half & half for desired spreading consistency in small bowl. Stir in 2 tablespoons chopped pistachio nuts.

• Spread bottoms of half of cookies with scant teaspoonful filling. Top with remaining cookies, bottom-side down.

Bittersweet Truffle Bites

Preparation time: **20 minutes** | Baking time: **8 minutes** | 96 bites

Crust

2 cups chocolate cookie crumbs
¼ cup sugar
½ cup LAND O LAKES® Butter, melted

Filling

6 (1-ounce) squares good quality bittersweet baking chocolate
1 (8-ounce) package cream cheese, softened
1 cup powdered sugar
½ cup LAND O LAKES™ Heavy Whipping Cream
1 tablespoon chocolate liqueur*

1 teaspoon unsweetened cocoa

• Heat oven to 375°F. Combine cookie crumbs and sugar in medium bowl; stir in melted butter. Pat onto bottom of ungreased 13×9-inch baking pan. Bake for 8 to 10 minutes or until set. Cool completely.

• Melt chocolate in 1-quart heavy saucepan over low heat; stir until smooth. Remove from heat. Cool slightly.

• Beat cream cheese at medium speed in large bowl until creamy. Add powdered sugar, whipping cream and liqueur; continue beating until well mixed. Increase speed to high. Beat for 2 minutes. Add melted chocolate; continue beating until well mixed. Spread over cooled crust. Refrigerate until firm (at least 2 hours).

• Sprinkle with cocoa powder. Refrigerate until serving time. Cut into small squares; place in mini foil baking cups. Store leftovers in refrigerator.

*Substitute 1 tablespoon vanilla.

tip:

Chocolate is a combination of cocoa butter, chocolate "liquor" (pressed liquid from roasted cocoa beans), and sugar. Imitation chocolates often substitute vegetable fats for the cocoa butter, making a product with less chocolate flavor.

Lemon Clove Cookie Sandwiches

Preparation time: **45 minutes** | Baking time: **8 minutes per pan** | **30 sandwich cookies**

Cookie

- ¾ cup LAND O LAKES® Butter, softened
- ¾ cup powdered sugar
- 1 egg
- ½ teaspoon lemon extract
- 1⅔ cups all-purpose flour
- ¼ teaspoon ground cloves
- ⅛ teaspoon salt

  Coarse-grain sugar

Filling

- 2½ cups powdered sugar
- ¼ cup LAND O LAKES® Butter, softened
- 2 tablespoons lemon juice
- ½ teaspoon lemon extract
- 1 to 2 tablespoons LAND O LAKES™ Fat Free Half & Half or milk

• Combine ¾ cup butter and ¾ cup powdered sugar in large bowl; beat at medium speed until creamy. Add egg and ½ teaspoon lemon extract; continue beating until combined. Reduce speed to low; add flour, cloves and salt.

• Divide dough in half; shape each half into 8-inch log. Wrap each in plastic food wrap. Refrigerate until firm (at least 2 hours).

• Heat oven to 350°F. Cut logs into ¼-inch slices with sharp knife. Place 1 inch apart onto ungreased cookie sheets. Sprinkle half of cookies with coarse sugar. Bake for 8 to 10 minutes or until edges begin to brown. Transfer to wire rack. Cool completely.

• Combine all filling ingredients in medium bowl, adding enough half & half for desired spreading consistency. Beat on low speed until well mixed.

• Spread about 1 teaspoon filling onto bottom of each cookie without sugar. Top with remaining cookies, sugar-side up.

Cranberry Orange Cookies

Preparation time: **30 minutes** | Baking time: **7 minutes per pan** | **5 dozen cookies**

Orange Sugar

⅓ cup sugar
1 teaspoon freshly grated orange peel

Cookie

1 cup sugar
¾ cup LAND O LAKES® Butter, softened
1 egg
2 cups all-purpose flour
1½ teaspoons baking powder
¼ teaspoon baking soda
½ cup sweetened dried cranberries, chopped
½ cup chopped macadamia nuts
1 tablespoon freshly grated orange peel

• Heat oven to 350°F. Combine all orange sugar ingredients in small bowl; stir until well mixed; set aside.

• Combine 1 cup sugar, butter and egg in large bowl; beat at medium speed until creamy. Reduce speed to low; add flour, baking powder and baking soda. Beat until well mixed. Add all remaining cookie ingredients. Continue beating just until mixed.

• Shape dough into 1-inch balls; roll balls in orange sugar. Place 2 inches apart onto ungreased cookie sheets. Flatten with bottom of glass to 1½-inch circles.

• Bake for 7 to 11 minutes or until edges are lightly browned. (DO NOT OVERBAKE.) Cool 1 minute; remove from cookie sheets.

tip:
To prevent cranberries from sticking to knife when chopping, spray knife with no-stick cooking spray.

tip:
To prevent hands from getting too sugary, shape dough into enough balls to fill 1 cookie sheet, then roll balls in orange sugar.

Peanut Butter Cookie Cups

Preparation time: **1 hour** | Baking time: **11 minutes per pan** | **4 dozen cookies**

- ½ cup sugar
- ½ cup firmly packed brown sugar
- ½ cup LAND O LAKES® Butter, softened
- ½ cup creamy peanut butter
- 1 egg
- ½ teaspoon vanilla
- 1¼ cups all-purpose flour
- ¾ teaspoon baking soda
- ¼ teaspoon salt
- 48 miniature peanut butter cups, unwrapped

• Heat oven to 350°F. Spray mini muffin pans with no-stick cooking spray; set aside.

• Combine sugar, brown sugar, butter and peanut butter in large bowl. Beat at medium speed, scraping bowl often, until creamy. Add egg and vanilla; continue beating until well mixed. Reduce speed to low; add flour, baking soda and salt. Beat, scraping bowl often, until well mixed.

• Shape dough into 1-inch balls. Place each ball into prepared mini muffin cup. Bake for 11 to 13 minutes or until lightly browned.

• Remove from oven; press peanut butter cup into center of each cookie. Cool 30 minutes. Remove from pans. Cool completely.

Drizzled Oatmeal Cookies

Preparation time: **30 minutes** | Baking time: **12 minutes per pan** | **2 dozen cookies**

Cookie

- 1 cup LAND O LAKES® Butter, softened
- 1 cup firmly packed brown sugar
- ¼ cup water
- 2½ cups uncooked old-fashioned or quick-cooking oats
- 1¼ cups all-purpose flour
- 1 teaspoon ground cinnamon
- ½ teaspoon baking soda
- ¼ teaspoon salt

Drizzle

- 1 cup powdered sugar
- 3 tablespoons unsweetened cocoa
- 1 teaspoon LAND O LAKES® Butter, softened
- 2 to 3 tablespoons milk

• Heat oven to 350°F. Combine 1 cup butter and brown sugar in large bowl. Beat at medium speed until creamy. Add water; continue beating until well mixed. Reduce speed to low; add oats, flour, cinnamon, baking soda and salt. Beat until well mixed.

• Shape dough into 1½-inch balls. (Dough will be sticky.) Place 2 inches apart onto ungreased cookie sheets. Flatten to 2-inch diameter with bottom of glass dipped in sugar. Bake for 12 to 15 minutes or until lightly browned. Let stand 1 minute; remove from cookie sheets. Cool completely.

• Combine all drizzle ingredients except milk in small bowl. Beat at low speed, gradually adding enough milk for desired drizzling consistency. Drizzle cooled cookies.

Chocolate Walnut Fudge

Preparation time: **10 minutes** | Cooking time: **12 minutes** | **9 dozen candies**

  4 cups sugar
  ½ cup LAND O LAKES® Butter
  1 (12-ounce) can evaporated milk
  2 (12-ounce) packages real semi-sweet chocolate chips
  1 (7-ounce) jar marshmallow crème
  2 cups chopped walnuts
  2 teaspoons vanilla

• Combine sugar, butter and evaporated milk in heavy 4-quart saucepan. Cook over medium heat, stirring occasionally, until mixture comes to a full boil (7 to 10 minutes). Continue cooking, stirring constantly, until candy thermometer reaches 228°F. (5 to 7 minutes).

• Remove from heat. Gradually stir in chocolate chips until melted. Stir in marshmallow crème until well mixed. Stir in nuts and vanilla.

• Spread fudge into lightly buttered 13×9-inch pan. Cool completely. Cut into 1-inch squares. Store refrigerated.

Old-Fashioned Molasses Cookies

Preparation time: **30 minutes** | Baking time: **8 minutes per pan** | **3 dozen cookies**

½ cup LAND O LAKES® Butter, softened
½ cup firmly packed brown sugar
¼ cup shortening
¾ cup molasses
1 egg
3 cups all-purpose flour
1 teaspoon baking soda
1 teaspoon ground cinnamon
½ teaspoon ground ginger
¼ teaspoon salt
¼ teaspoon ground cloves

Sugar

• Combine butter, brown sugar, shortening, molasses and egg in large bowl. Beat at medium speed, scraping bowl often, until creamy. Reduce speed to low; add all remaining ingredients except sugar. Beat until well mixed. Cover; refrigerate until firm (1 to 2 hours).

• Heat oven to 375°F. Shape dough into 1½-inch balls; roll in sugar. Place 2 inches apart onto ungreased cookie sheets. Flatten balls with bottom of glass dipped in sugar. Bake for 8 to 11 minutes or until set.

Maple Cashew Brittle

Preparation time: **10 minutes** | Cooking time: **14 minutes** | 3 dozen pieces

- 1 cup firmly packed brown sugar
- ¾ cup maple-flavored syrup
- ¼ cup LAND O LAKES® Butter (no substitutions)
- 1 cup lightly salted cashew halves
- ½ teaspoon baking soda

• Butter large baking sheet; set aside. Combine brown sugar and syrup in 2-quart heavy saucepan. Cook over medium heat, stirring occasionally, until sugar is dissolved and mixture comes to a full boil (4 to 9 minutes).

• Add butter; continue cooking, stirring occasionally, until candy thermometer reaches 300°F. or small amount of mixture dropped into ice water forms a hard brittle strand (10 to 18 minutes).

• Remove from heat; stir in cashews and baking soda. Immediately pour mixture onto prepared baking sheet, spreading evenly to ⅛- to ¼-inch thickness. Cool completely. Break into pieces. Store in container with tight-fitting lid.

ITALIAN

METRIC CONVERSION CHART

VOLUME MEASUREMENTS (dry)

$\frac{1}{8}$ teaspoon = 0.5 mL
$\frac{1}{4}$ teaspoon = 1 mL
$\frac{1}{2}$ teaspoon = 2 mL
$\frac{3}{4}$ teaspoon = 4 mL
1 teaspoon = 5 mL
1 tablespoon = 15 mL
2 tablespoons = 30 mL
$\frac{1}{4}$ cup = 60 mL
$\frac{1}{3}$ cup = 75 mL
$\frac{1}{2}$ cup = 125 mL
$\frac{2}{3}$ cup = 150 mL
$\frac{3}{4}$ cup = 175 mL
1 cup = 250 mL
2 cups = 1 pint = 500 mL
3 cups = 750 mL
4 cups = 1 quart = 1 L

VOLUME MEASUREMENTS (fluid)

1 fluid ounce (2 tablespoons) = 30 mL
4 fluid ounces ($\frac{1}{2}$ cup) = 125 mL
8 fluid ounces (1 cup) = 250 mL
12 fluid ounces (1$\frac{1}{2}$ cups) = 375 mL
16 fluid ounces (2 cups) = 500 mL

WEIGHTS (mass)

$\frac{1}{2}$ ounce = 15 g
1 ounce = 30 g
3 ounces = 90 g
4 ounces = 120 g
8 ounces = 225 g
10 ounces = 285 g
12 ounces = 360 g
16 ounces = 1 pound = 450 g

DIMENSIONS

$\frac{1}{16}$ inch = 2 mm
$\frac{1}{8}$ inch = 3 mm
$\frac{1}{4}$ inch = 6 mm
$\frac{1}{2}$ inch = 1.5 cm
$\frac{3}{4}$ inch = 2 cm
1 inch = 2.5 cm

OVEN TEMPERATURES

250°F = 120°C
275°F = 140°C
300°F = 150°C
325°F = 160°C
350°F = 180°C
375°F = 190°C
400°F = 200°C
425°F = 220°C
450°F = 230°C

BAKING PAN SIZES

Utensil	Size in Inches/Quarts	Metric Volume	Size in Centimeters
Baking or Cake Pan (square or rectangular)	8 × 8 × 2	2 L	20 × 20 × 5
	9 × 9 × 2	2.5 L	23 × 23 × 5
	12 × 8 × 2	3 L	30 × 20 × 5
	13 × 9 × 2	3.5 L	33 × 23 × 5
Loaf Pan	8 × 4 × 3	1.5 L	20 × 10 × 7
	9 × 5 × 3	2 L	23 × 13 × 7
Round Layer Cake Pan	8 × 1½	1.2 L	20 × 4
	9 × 1½	1.5 L	23 × 4
Pie Plate	8 × 1¼	750 mL	20 × 3
	9 × 1¼	1 L	23 × 3
Baking Dish or Casserole	1 quart	1 L	—
	1½ quarts	1.5 L	—
	2 quarts	2 L	—